NORWEGIAN BUNADS

NORWEGIAN BUNADS

English edition by Bent Vanberg
Norwegian text Kjersti Skavhaug
Pictures Arne Svendsen a.o.

Published by
HJEMMENES FORLAG
OSLO, NORWAY

Printed in Spain by Mateu Cromo, S.A. 1982
4. edition ISBN 82-7006-177-8

FOREWORD

This book is intended as a follow-up of the previous, now out-of-print edition of the publisher's «*VÅRE VAKRE BUNADER*» («OUR BEAUTIFUL BUNADS»). This time, too, we present only a selection of bunads from all provinces of the country. We have chosen festive bunads as they appear today. The «Same» or Lapp costumes have not been included, because they belong to another geographic and cultural sphere than Norwegian bunads. Altogether there are probably a couple of hundred different bunads in this country, but hardly anyone has a complete listing of them all. As it would have been impractical to present all the bunads in this volume, bunads not pictured are dealt with in the provincial areas section.

Primarily, representative bunads from all the provinces are shown. Some regions have a rich folk costume tradition and numerous bunads. In the province of Finnmark, however, we know of no folk costume tradition among the non-samic population, and that province has only one single bunad.

Our intention has, above all, been to present bunads built on a folk costume tradition yet without this principle having determined the selection of bunads. When describing the individual bunads we have tried to point to the relationship between the bunad of today and the local folk costume tradition, and also to provide concrete information about those who took the initiative to the design of reconstructed bunads, when the bunads came into use, and the background material relied on, in short, to provide a glimpse of the bunad history itself.

The access to information about the folk costume traditions and the bunad works of recent dates vary from locale to locale, which will be in evidence as for some of the bunad descriptions. By and large, the information is provided by the literature registered by the Costume Bibliography of 1976, published by the «Landsnemnda for Bunadspørsmål», «THE NATIONAL BUNAD COMMITTEE».

We thank «Landsnemnda for Bunadspørsmål» for cordial assistance by placing their extensive records of Norwegian bunads at our disposal. We particularly thank Aagot Noss for valuable advice and for making available her costume research material and viewpoints on folk costumes and bunads through books, articles and lectures.

We would also like to thank everyone throughout the country, who has assisted us with information and corrections as for the description of the various bunads, and helped us to find suitable photo models with top class bunads. We extend profound thanks to Ranveig Bakke, Sverre Berg, Berit Berget, Elsa Bjerck, Olga Breivik, The Bunad Committee of Voss Youth Society, Anna Lund, «Bærum Husflidsforening», Helga Doseth, Ragnhild Fossum, Ragnhild Glad, Målfrid Grimstvedt, Eli Gulla, Peder Gullikstad, Rannveig Nybø Hagane, «Husfliden i Alta», «Husfliden i Bergen» (Martha Omvik), «Husfliden i Kristiansund», «Husfliden i Namsos», «Husfliden i Oslo» (Tone Huus), «Husfliden i Trondheim» (Johanna Hoel Erichsen), «Husfliden i Valle» (Agnes Smith), «Husfliden i Voss», Øydis Eide Høyland, Nilsine Kallestad, Magny Smedsrud Karlberg, Turid Gislerud Liodden, Inger Miland, Mathilde Myhra, Sigrid Norehaugen, Torbjørg Aamlid Paus, Gunhild Wøllo Ransedokken, Ingebjørg Rydland, Johanna Røen, Eva Wahl Sandnes, Elvine Skarvikeng, Kari Stangnes, Gudrun Stuland, «Sunnmøre frilyndt Ungdomslag» (Rune Håndlykken), «Sunnmøre Husflidslag», Kjellaug Tverrdal, Eva Woldmo, Viktor Winnberg, Tove Østby, «Østfold Husflidslag», and all others who so kindly assisted us.

Kjersti Skavhaug,
Oslo, Norway.

BUNADS

The bunads as we now know them and use them belong to this century. The word *bunad* simply means clothes. But in everyday Norwegian language a bunad is a festive costume tied to a specific area and with ancient traditions behind it.

In Norway the woman's bunad is used on festive occasions, in the family circle at christenings, confirmations and weddings, and at representations and public ceremonies. The interest in our bunads began with the folk dancing movement at the beginning of this century. In the circles around folk dancing and folk music the use of bunads is a matter of course for the women as well as the men. This is also the case in a number of other countries, but the general use of the woman's bunad by all seems to be a uniquely Norwegian custom.

Some contemporary bunads cover a whole «fylke» (province), such as Østfold, Rogaland and Finnmark, while in a single valley, such as Hallingdal, one may find several different bunads. Traditionally, there has never been a single costume covering such a large area as a «fylke», yet the area has normally been larger than a parish or township.

Many of our bunads are not very old as for their present appearance. Most of them have been reconstructed or composed in this century by individuals or bunad committees wishing to preserve or revive an old, local tradition. In some places, such as in Setesdal, Hardanger and Numedal, the traditional festive costumes from old days are still used, even if the people there wear modern everyday clothes. These bunads are the last link in the development of the folk costume. The folk costumes were far more varied, in shape as well as use, than the bunads of today.

Other bunads have been copied from old folk costumes no longer in use. Still we know them so well that we are well acquainted with how they looked like and how and when they were used. Those bunads we designate as «traditional in origin».

Some bunads, however, are composed on the basis of meager and uncertain historical data. It is not certain whether all parts of the country have had their own regional folk costumes. In many areas it has been difficult to single out such costumes. Where no complete costume was found one has tried to find a single piece of clothing which could be used as a starting point for a bunad with some linkage with the area.

There is no reason to hide the fact that some bunads became so popular as to serve as models for various new bunads, such as the flower-embroidered Gudbrandsdal bunads. We have areas where they preferred to make such a bunad rather than copying old, local folk costumes not meeting the taste of time. There are also bunads not based on local historical costume records at all. The bunad embroideries may be based on rose-painted furniture, meadow flowers and embroideries which previously never adorned any garment.

Consequently, today's bunads have very diversified backgrounds. Not all are equally old, not all stem from the costume customs of earlier eras. Thus, it is important that the bunad saga becomes known, that is, the history of the effort to revive the customs of centuries past and search for local festive costumes. It is important that this history be written, providing us with the history of every single bunad.

As the old folk costume traditions are maintained through the bunads, so does the bunad work ensure a continuation of the old traditions in material qualities, cuts and sewing techniques. Quality is a byword in the bunad work. Much of the finest handworks we have in our country comes from old clothes. We particularly have in mind the genuine Hardanger embroidery with the fine geometric patterns embroidered with white linen thread on fine, white linen on neckbands and aprons have doily woven bands. In some areas the yarn has been plant-dyed in order to obtain the correct color nuances.

The bunad saga is a saga of this century. It shows how our bunads are a result of thoughts and trends in our time and also a continuation of old traditions. It is also the history of many years of eagerness and enterprising work in search of the bunads to make them known and loved.

HULDA GARBORG (1862—1934)

Hulda Garborg's excellent work for the folk dance became at the same time the start of the bunad work in this country. At the end of the last century, she started a «leikarring» in the capital. At first a group of Kristiania (Oslo) ladies got together and danced. Around 1900 the «leikarring» gave its first performance in the «Bondeungdomslaget» in Kristiania, and thus the folk song dances came alive. Hulda Garborg was asked to give dance instructions in many parts of the country, and her group also performed outside Norway. During the first period almost all the performing women used the «national costume», a simplified version of the Hardanger costume. Hulda Garborg, however, wore her own version of the Halling costume. In the beginning only a few of the male dancers wore bunads from their home areas.

Hulda Garborg in her version of the Gol bunad.

Hulda Garborg authored the first bunad book in Norway. It was «Norsk Klædebunad», published in 1903. In 1917 it appeared in a new, expanded edition. The book was mainly intended as a help for those who wanted to acquire other bunads than the «Hardanger National». «Good and suitable bunads are still available», she wrote in 1917. «The question is how to bring them out into the open again», she added. Nationwide, the people got the idea. Why wear an inferior copy of the Hardanger costume when they could use the costumes from their own home areas? The need of the folk dancers to wear suitable costumes when in action, stimulated the bunad work in many districts.

Hulda Garborg was extremely occupied by reforms of the «Heimestellet», which to her was far more than just «housekeeping work». She maintained that one had to build on the good, simple customs which still flourished in the valleys. But they had to be adapted to our time. She viewed the bunads in the same way. She found that many of the old costumes, as they had been, were too unwieldy. Changes and alterations were required. It is not always easy to follow Hulda Garborg's ideas for reforms. When she made «a sleeveless Finn bunad for use at home» then not much was left of the form or use of the Same jacket. And when the Gol bunad lost its apron, the width of the skirt and was given long instead of short suspenders, it became quite a different costume. It is easier to understand her when she says that «in rural Norway we need solid and warm clothes». Also a part of Hulda Garborg's reform program was her encouragement of people to use homespun, Norwegian materials. In the foreword to «Norsk Klædebunad» she quotes the proverbs that «the one who wears homespun clothes does not spend more than he earns», and «velvet patch does not belong on homespun trousers». Yet, she was aware of the fact that our domestic bunads were a part of clothes and fashions in Continental Europe.

Hulda Garborg's bunad efforts have to be seen in the context of her overall work to bring out and build on the rural culture. She herself was from the district of Hedmark, and in Kristiania she

Hulda Garborg's Folk Dance Group of 1902. (From an old postcard).

switched to the «New Norwegian» language. The folk dances and the bunads constituted one side of the national activities she took part in. She also founded the Norwegian Fiddlers' Society, which later became The Norwegian Theater. In the beginning, the Fiddlers' Society often accompanied the folk dancers after the performances at the theater when it was touring the country. Thus people became acquainted with the folk song dance and the bunads used by the dancers.

Today it sounds unbelievable, but the dancers who participated in the original «leikarrings», were often mobbed in the capital city when they walked around in their bunads. On the other hand, it gives us a measure of the pioneer work done by Hulda Garborg and others.

KLARA SEMB (1884—1970)

In 1902 Klara Semb was one of the dancers in Hulda Garborg's «Leikarring» at the Skansen in Stockholm, Sweden, and for a while she was an actress at The Norwegian Theatre. But gradually it was the work of Hulda Garborg for the folk dancing and the bunads she carried on. While Hulda Garborg's interest in bunads was only one side of her authorship and work, bunads, in addition to folk dance, became the main, lifelong task for Klara Semb. Originally, she was a city girl from Kristiania. As a young person she became associated with nationalist and patriotic circles, and gradually she found her language form in the «New Norwegian» (nynorsk).

Since early in the century she criss-crossed the country as a dance instructor. That way she acquired a unique knowledge of the various bunads. Numerous people have been assisted and inspired by her in their work on local bunads, and there are still many around who can tell about their cooperation with Klara Semb. Unfortunately she has not written much about bunads, except during the years 1922—32. She was then the editor of the column «På leikvollen» in the publication «For bygd og by». And in the special address honoring her on her 80th birthday in 1946 she states:

«At an early stage I saw it as a goal to get rid of the objectionable, modernized bunads and bring back the stylish, genuine bunads both with regard to material, colors, lines, embroideries, silver jewelry, caps, etc. Gradually the rural people began to show an interest. It took a long time before people generally began to understand and appreciate this work, but now they do, and the bunads are improving all the time.»

To her quality was essential. Those who worked with her say she was very strict in her insistence that old clothes be copied with great care. In contrast to Hulda Garborg, Klara Semb said foreign materials had to be used in addition to the homespun ones. When «The Landsnemnda for Bunadspørsmål» («The National Committee for Bunads») was established in 1947, it was selfevident that Klara Semb became one of its members, and she served as such until 1965.

Klara Semb in her Østerdal bunad.

«LANDSNEMNDA FOR BUNADSPØRSMÅL» «THE NATIONAL BUNADS COMMITTEE»

In Norway we have a state institution dealing with bunad matters, «Landsnemnda for Bunadspørsmål», established in 1947. Klara Semb was a member of that committee and initially its work was very much influenced by her ideas. Gradually the committee changed somewhat. One should bear in mind that the committee was formed right after the war when it was somewhat of a problem to obtain quality materials for bunad sewing. Much of the work during those first years went into evaluation of the material samples obtained, and providing the producers with quality fabrics. This is still a part of the activities of the committee as it advices on the suitability of the materials for bunads. The committee has built up a record collection of samples of fabrics, ribbons, etc. to assist in this work. It also publishes information about technical assistance for sewing and mounting of bunads.

The initial work program included the following:

1. «The Committee shall try to support the bunad tradition in those areas of the country where it is still alive, and prevent abuses. It shall provide practical advice for restoration of the old bunads or creation of new details of an old bunad.
2. «The Committee gives advise on reconstruction of bunads based on traditional folk costumes in those districts where the bunad tradition is minor, or in the process of dying.
3. «The Committee evaluates proposals for newly created bunads in districts where the tradition has completely disappeared.»

Following new statutes adopted in 1967, the committee's program was somewhat altered. Now the committee only deals with reconstruction of bunads based on traditional folk costumes. It no longer gives advice for new bunad creations. One has taken the consequences of the viewpoint, that the only factual basis for a reconstruction of bunads can build on, is the history of our folk costumes. Since the costume research provides us with more knowledge of the folk costumes, it is only natural that the demands on the background material for the bunad, are made more rigorous. One demand is that the bunad should be a copy of the folk costume as it was in use at a certain period of time. Folk costume fashions also have changed. When one wants to take into use an old costume, one must be certain that the various pieces really belong together.

One problem facing those who handle bunads, is the difference between *genuine* and *non-genuine* bunads, *approved* and *non-approved* bunads. Hulda Garborg, as well as Klara Semb, discuss authentic folk costumes without attaching any precise meaning of the term. Before the Committee adopted the new statutes in 1967, it took positions on a number of reconstructions and new creations of bunads. The bunads recommended by the Committee were regarded as «approved», and those bunads considered not good enough, or in need of improvements, were characterized as «not approved».

The Committe can not, of course, dictate the design of a bunad, but it renders assistance and evaluates the end product. A considerable part of the Committee's work consists of helping make the bunad reconstructions be as true to the folk costume tradition as possible. Some bunad proposals are rejected because they do not build on the traditional costume material. Some of the bunads «approved» prior to 1967 would not be acceptable today. Quite a few bunads have never been submitted to the Committee for approval.

The Committee has a substantial archive covering all kinds of Norwegian bunads, it issues brochures about the usage of bunads, and a bibliography on the subject. This is revised annually, and may be obtained without cost.

ORGANIZATIONS

For many years a number of large organizations have been active in bunad work. Already in the 1890s «national costumes» were sold at «Den Norske Husflidsforening» store in Kristiania. Later most home-handicraft stores in the country have sold bunads and materials for bunad sewing. Some home crafts societies have, since the turn of the century, offered courses in bunad sewing.

During the 1920s bunad committees were appointed in local and district chapters of the Norwegian Youth Association. In the 1970s this organization formed its own national committee to take care of bunad matters. This committee must not be confused with the committee dealt with in the previous chapter.

«Bondeungdomslaget i Oslo» («The Farm Youth Society in Oslo») opened its own store,

«Heimen», in 1925, making and selling bunads. Locally, «Noregs Bondekvinnelag» («Farm Women Society») and «Norges Husmorlag» («Norway's Homemakers' Society») have formed their own bunad committees, or are being represented in such committees. In some areas several organizations have joined forces to create or redesign bunads. Those organizations are also conducting courses. «Noregs Bondekvinnelag» has, in addition, registered textiles throughout the country. In that way old costume materials have come to light.

Setesdal is one of the districts where the folk costume tradition has stayed alive up until today. This amateur picture shows a chance meeting of city women on a hiking trip and Setesdal women in their everyday attire in Valle in 1911. It is said that the local women expressed their dissatisfaction with the modern sports attire of the city women, particularly their pants.

THE FOLK COSTUME

The words *bunad* and *folk costume* are too often mixed up. It might be worthwhile to distinguish between them, as has been done for several years in costume research. *Bunad* is the festive costume used by us today, more or less similar to the costume in use in olden times in the geographical area where it originated. As for the *folk costume*, we think of the everyday and holiday clothes worn in a specific area. But in order to designate it as a folk costume, it must be different from the costumes used in the neighboring districts and in the cities. The folk costumes have been in regular use only in a few parts of the country in this century. In Kristiania and in Kongsberg, it has been possible up until today to recognize the Setesdal and Flesberg women by their costume. But it was mainly during the last century, and earlier, that our folk costumes were used.

Garments for various use
Folk costumes included all types of garments, from work clothes to the finest festive ones, and for all seasons. In earlier times one was more strict in separating everyday garments from holiday

clothes. It also happened that the holiday garments were completely worn out through everyday use. Far into this century the church has been the focal point of rural community life. It was in the churchyard people met. The garments then worn were always the very finest ones. But there was also a difference between the costumes worn on a regular Sunday and on special holidays. Some garments were only worn inside the church. In Sotra, the women arrived with small boxes containing a kerchief and shoulder shawl, which they put on before entering the church. In Røros, during the last century, they had a special costume for communion. Everywhere the very finest garments were worn for weddings, and the bridal couple had their very own costumes.

Difference between people

In many places the dresses separated the married people from the unmarried. Normally the unmarried women would wear their hair uncovered, or with a ribbon tied to it. The married women always had to have a head cover, either a kerchief, cap or hood. It was an old unwritten «law», that the girls were not to dress up as much as the wives. Silver belts were also called «wife belts». In Setesdal, however, it was the young ones, who were to have «løye» embroideries on their costumes, while the older ones were to settle for something less. It is also clear that the garment customs in the old days marked the difference between the prominent people and the common people, even if we do not know much about that. It is an open question whether we have not been left with a distorted picture of how the folk costumes really looked like, because most often it is the finest garments which have been preserved, and they are the ones ordinarily used in illustrations.

Origin

We are not going to discuss the question of the origin of our folk costumes. It is quite certain that they are connected with the European fashion garments. But the road from the Spanish court and Paris to Setesdal and Gudbrandsdalen may have been a long and very winding one. And when a European costume fashion found its way into a Norwegian valley and was accepted, it was adapted to the local conditions. This is believed to be the way that folk costumes came into being: something came from the outside world, something was created locally, and the result was costumes which had something in common with costumes from other areas, while at the same time having a distinct character of their own. Not all of the folk costumes, however, have had a common historic development. Thus we cannot transfer what we know about one costume into the history of another. The fact that two costumes resemble each other, does not necessarily mean that they have an identical origin or development. The french empire style was fashionable in France in the beginning of the 19th C. The «Empire costume» appeared in Flå only in the second half of the last century. The women's costumes with a very short bodice in Øvre Hallingdal and Setesdal, on the other hand, are older than the French «Empire costume», and cannot, in spite of the similarity, have any connection with it.

Today costume research is very preoccupid with a thorough review of the costume areas, what the folk costumes looked like throughout the country, and when they were in use in the various districts, more than in the efforts to find connections with European fashion trends.

Costume regions

A folk costume was worn in large or small districts, with clearly definable borderlines: a costume district. Setesdal, for example, constitutes such an area. In addition, inside Setesdal one again finds minor differences between the Valle and Bykle costume customs. The same goes for well known costume districts such as Sogn and Hardanger, where the individual valleys have their own characteristic designs. Generally, one may say that a district («fylke»), is too large and incongruous an area to constitute a costume district. On the other hand, one single rural community is too small. Thus, today we have many bunads, which do not fall within the borderlines of the old costume districts.

Costumes were varied

It has hardly ever been a rule that everybody within a community must wear completely uniform costumes. On the contrary, it was up to every single individual to apply different colors, fabrics and ornamentations, within certain limits. As an example, a private person in Hardanger collected more than 600 different old plastrons. Most of the garments were in the old days made at home. What was added through buying of clothes and jewelry varied, depending on what was available. In many places it was customary that the tailors did the men's costumes while specialists handled the more intricate details of the festive costumes for the women. In Telemark one may still find the names of the women and men who made the extra fine embroideries on the women's as well as the men's costumes.

«Girls from Kvinnherad». Photograph by Marcus Selmer, Bergen, published 1872.

Folk costume fashions changed

While fashions changed quite rapidly in the cities and among the «upper classes» in the countryside, the folk costumes remained comparatively unchanged. Still, fashions also changed in the rural districts. In several districts we find older as well as younger folk costume types. This book contains several examples showing that both older and younger folk costumes inside the same area have been reestablished as the bunad of today (Numedal, Telemark, Røros). As a rule the male costume types changed more often than the female types. The folk costumes were used within a rural community and the public opinion regulated how the costume and the single garbs were to look. The older generations knew best.

Many of our bunads are built on the folk costumes as they were in use during the last century. Some costumes and garments may be traced even further back. What separates the bunads from the folk costumes is that the bunads have achieved a final form which will not become outdated. They are used on festive occasions, and are consequently not the dresses for everyday use, as the folk costumes were. They changed as time went by, although quite slowly. The folk costume consisted of several pieces of garment for various uses. In addition, not all the costumes from one and the same area were quite alike, but varied according to personal taste.

WHAT DO WE KNOW ABOUT OUR FOLK COSTUMES?

What did they look like? How were they used? When were the various folk costumes worn? These are the questions the costume researchers try to answer for us.

Costume material

The most reliable sources of information we have, are of course in the rural areas where the folk costume tradition has been preserved up to now. There we find preserved costumes as well as people, who can tell about the costume customs. Old garments kept intact in the homes and at the museums tell us how people were dressed in the old days. The garments themselves are, therefore, an important source of knowledge of the folk costumes. If we are to copy those old garments it becomes absolutely necessary to have them at hand. Only then are we able to determine the fabric, quality, the cut and the sewing. Yet, preserved costume material is often quite widely scattered. Far more single garments than complete costumes are preserved, and they may date back to different time periods. We also lack information about many such garments. It proves difficult both to date them and to know with which other pieces of garment they were worn.

Folk costume pictures

In addition to the costumes themselves the illustrations of folk costumes also show how the attire looked like. They are, therefore, essential for an understanding of the preserved costume material. During the last century several Norwegian artists drew and painted folk costumes. Some of these pictures were later printed and published as collections. J. F. L. Dreier (1775—1833) of Trøndelag drew folk costumes from his area, Østerdalen and Vestlandet around 1800. Only with the publication of Einar Lexow's book in 1931 about Dreier's folk costume water colors, it became clear that some of his pictures have been models for the copperplate engravings of Johannes Senn. They were published in Copenhagen in 1810—12 under the title «Norwegian National Costumes». Johannes Flintoe (1787—1870) drew and painted folk costumes primarily from the Østlandet valleys, but also from Hardanger, Sogn, Trøndelag and Finnmark. Flintoe's folk costume pictures appeared in the years 1819—30. Joachim Frich (1810—50) concentrated on the Vestlandet folk costumes, as did the publisher G. C. Prahl in Bergen. He issued two series of Norwegian folk costumes by different artists: «Norway's Most Unique Peasant Costumes» in 1828—30, and «Norwegian Peasant Costumes» in 1848. In Christiania the collection «Norwegian National Costumes» was published by Christian Tønsberg in 1852. These prints too had the pictures by various artists as motifs, among them Johan Fredrik Eckersberg (1822—70). In addition to the artists, who specialized in folk costumes, we have several others who made excellent costume studies when preparing for larger paintings, such as Adolph Tidemand (1814—76), and Erik Werenskiold (1855—1938).

The costume researcher Aagot Noss has, through her works on Johannes Flintoe and Joachim Frich, shown that the artists often «borrowed» motifs from each other. She indicates that very often the same model appears in folk costume pictures by different artists. Several pictures of one single folk costume may be accepted as proof that the costume has existed.

Photographs

During the second half of the last century photographers began to show an interest in folk costumes. The best known older photo collections are those by photographers A. B. Wilse, at the Norwegian Folk Museum, and M. Selmer at the Historical Museum in Bergen. It would be wrong, however, to think of photos as completely reliable sources. In those times, as now, it was

Along with the national romance of the mid-1800s the interest in our folk costumes also came alive. In the 1870s—80s it became fashionable for women throughout the country to wear national costumes. Most fashionable was the Hardanger costume, which also was called the «Hardanger National», or the «National» only. Even in rural areas, where they already had a distinct local folk costume tradition, the «Hardanger National» became very popular. It was mostly a very simplified and rough copy of the traditional festive bunad from Hardanger, with a red bodice and dark skirt. White shirt sleeves and a white apron, often with a very rough Hardanger embroidery, also were a «must». The romantic view on the national costume also appears on old postcards, showing women in national costumes milking goats and raking hay. The national costume also played a certain part as a national symbol in political matters, such as the flag issue. While one in the last century were searching for a *national* trait, in our century we are increasingly concerned with the *local* ones, which the bunad movement exemplifies. (From old postcards.)

common practice to retouch pictures. In addition, the photographers also had standard equipment, such as background scenery, props, even complete costumes worn by occasional models. Portraits of people being photographed in their regular clothes are perhaps a more reliable source for knowledge about folk costumes, than the series of folk costume pictures by the photographers.

Sculpture

We also have sculptures featuring Norwegian folk costumes. In the 1760s the Palace Park, Nordmandsdalen, at the Fredensborg Castle in North Zealand, Denmark, was constructed, with statues of Norwegian and Faroese farmers dressed in their special costumes. The statues are the works by the Danish artist Johan G. Grund (1733—96). But the models for all the Norwegian figures are some small ivory statuettes, carved by Jørgen Garnaas of Hallingdal (1723—98). He is also the creator of a collection of wooden dolls with folk costumes, now at the Historical Museum in Bergen.

Literature

The Norwegian folk costume literature is very extensive, covering the whole range from voluminous monographs and publications to numerous articles in rural books and magazines. Older topographical descriptions often included a chapter about the costume customs, and foreigners writing travel articles about Norway, often described the folk costumes.

Probates

Old probates are an important and widely used source of knowledge about the costume customs in earlier times. But while the probate records provide us with detailed information about fabrics, colors and the names of the individual garments, they tell very little about the sewing itself and the shape of the clothes, and nothing about which garments were worn together.

Thanks to various sources we know quite a lot about some of the Norwegian folk costumes. On the other hand, there are areas of the country with no folk costume tradition at all, as far as we know. This may be due to the fact that not all areas had their own folk costumes. Only a thorough registration of preserved costume material and pictures will provide us with a complete record of how the folk costumes throughout the nation looked like.

ØSTFOLD

Østfold was one of the first districts to change from the local folk costumes to garments of a more modern design. The traditional folk costumes were probably in use until about 1800, and there is reason to belive that the costumes varied from area to area in Østfold.

The new Østfold bunad was displayed at the Østfold Fair in 1930. It was copied after an antique skirt and bodice with a peplum, from Ellefsrød in Idd. In 1936 the Østfold Husflidslag appointed a committee to continue the work on a bunad for Østfold. The result is the costume they use today. «Den Norske Husflidsforening» in Oslo designed a variation of the bunad. They are still working on a man's bunad, having started on it in 1960. Antique clothes from Ellefsrød in Idd, dated about 1800, are being used as models. The so-called «Løkendrakten» from 1946 was designed by architect Halvdan Arneberg. The embroidery is copied after a cupboard from Lille Løken in Trøgstad.

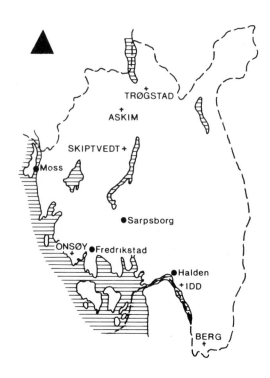

Frå Folkemuseet, Interiör fra Smaalenene

«From Smaalenene». Postcard from one-man exhibit of national costumes at the Norwegian Folk Museum in 1903.

Woman's bunad from Østfold

This bunad was designed in 1936 by a bunad committee appointed by Østfold Husflidslag. The idea for the bunad was picked up particularly from antique clothes and fabrics found in different parts of Østfold.

The embroidery on the shawl, cap and purse was copied from a silk scarf pattern found at Ellefsrød in Idd, originally bought in Valdres in the 19th C. The old scarf has embroidery on two of its corners. It is the same pattern, but one corner has mainly green embroidery, while the other has red. But for this bunad the green embroidery was chosen. Instead of the red embroidery the bunad's shawl has a little rose that originally was a pattern on a scarf found in Askim. The cap's design is a copy of an old cap found in Bossum, Onsøy, dated about 1830. The whitework on the blouse was copied from a man's shirt, dated about 1840, also from Bossum.

A little silver pin from Onsøy became the design for the eyelets on each side of the bodice. The brooch is supposed to be a copy of a brooch from Rakkestad. The pattern on the purse-closing was stamped by an old goldsmith from Fredrikstad, in the mid-19th C. The skirt is made of black wool, bordered at the hem with two different colored bands, one wide band in green or rust with two thin red bands above. The skirt is finely pleated. The bodice material is wool, either in green or rust with «Spruce-tree» pattern. The blouse is made of white linen. It has whitework on the shoulder-parts, the high standing collar and cuffs of the sleeves.

The cap is made of black silk and it has the same embroidery as the shawl and purse. The black silk shawl has a variety of colors in the embroidery, placed in one of the shawl's corners, the opposite corner has a little rose in blue and white.

The purse is made of the same material as the skirt, and it has the same embroidery as the cap and shawl. The purse buckle is made of silver or silverplate. Black stockings and black shoes are part of the costume. The bunad's silver consists of a chain and eyelets for the bodice, a little ring-shaped neckpin and a bigger brooch with dangles, all especially designed for this bunad. We use a short reversible cape for the outdoors. One side is black and the other green. It joins at the neckline with a silver or brass clasp.

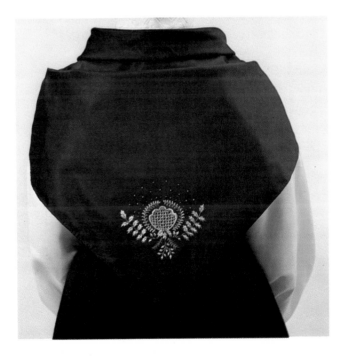

Woman's bunad from Østfold

This is a variation of the Østfold bunad from the preceding page. It was designed by Den Norske Husflidsforening in Oslo.

The old silk-embroidered scarf from Ellefsrød in Idd, originally from Valdres, is also the model for the shawl belonging to this bunad. For this particular variation, they used the copy of the scarf's side that had the red embroidery. They also gave this bunad an apron, copied after a hand-woven, half woolen material from Skiptvet. The red cap was modeled after an old cap from Ellefsrød. The skirt is made of black wool from «spelsaugarn», bordered at the hem with two different colored bands, one wide green band and above this a thin, red band. The skirt is finely pleated, and it has an inserted pocket on one side. The bodice is made of green or rust colored wool with «Spruce-tree» pattern, and it has lacing in front.

The blouse is made of white linen with whitework on part of the shoulders, around the high standing collar and cuffs on the sleeves. The cap's material is red silk with pink silk ribbon and white lace edging, it has a long, pink silk ribbon that can be tied. The shawl is made of black silk with silk embroidery placed in one of the shawl's corners, done in a variety of colors. The widestriped designed apron is made of half woolen material. Black stockings and black shoes are part of the costume. We use a short reversible cape for the outdoors, one side is black the other is green. It joins at the neckline with a silver or brass clasp. The bunad's silver consists of silver eyelets and chain, a little ring-shaped pin in silver and a bigger brooch, all designed especially for this bunad.

AKERSHUS

There is very little information available about the traditional folk costume from Akershus, and it is not known if there ever existed any particular costume in or around the Capital. None of the artists who painted pictures of folk costumes from the last century, made any pictures from Akershus. And very little is written about the traditional costumes. Eilert Sundt wrote about the use of the costumes at Romerike in the middle of the last century. He stated that there was a big difference between rich and poor, but he did not really explain what the costumes looked like. In the book «Urskogs Beskrivelse» from 1882, Anders Heyerdal describes both the woman's and man's costumes from Aurskog, from about 1800. His description of the woman's costume was partly used as a basis for the woman's bunad designed in 1936.

Today's woman's bunad from Romerike comes in several variations. The man's bunad was designed in 1952. Right after the Second World War «Bondekvinnelagene» and «Husflidslagene», began to design bunads for Bærum, Asker and Follo. The Asker bunad was completed in 1962, the following year the Bærum bunad was completed, and in 1970 Follo had it's own bunad. All the three costumes are copied after antique garments and materials from different areas of Akershus.

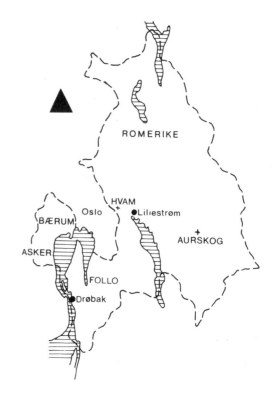

Rejer Gielleból: «Natural and economic description of the Høland parish. Akershus district of Norway».
Copenhagen 1771.

Woman's bunad from Romerike

The first Romerike bunad was designed in the 1930s. Later we have had some variations of the woman's bunad. It may be made of red, blue or green colored material. Some have bodice with a peplum, others have waist-band, then others again have brocade bodice, and some are made of the same material, and have the same embroidery as the skirt. Also, the embroidery varies. The bunad that is shown in the pictures, was designed by Borghild Tranum Røer in cooperation with «Heimen», about 1942—1946. The bodice design was a copy from an antique bodice from Sørum, dated about 1760—1770. The hat's pattern comes from the same place. An antique purse-pattern was used to design the purse. The embroidery is a copy from a saddle blanket from Enebakk, dated about 1730.

This is one variation of the Romerike bunad: The skirt is made of blue-green colored wool material, and is bordered at the hem with a red band, and the embroidery is made in golden colored wool yarn. The skirt is pleated. It has a bodice with a peplum, made of the same material as the skirt. The bodice has a thin, red, border stripe. It has the same wool yarn embroidery as the skirt has. The bodice has lacing in front. The blouse is made of white linen with whitework around the collar and cuffs of the sleeves. The hat is made of the same material as the rest of the bunad. It has embroidery in golden colored wool yarn, the same as the purse, with purse closing made of brass or silver. Black stockings and black shoes are part of the costume. The bunad's silver consists of silver eyelets for the bodice, button cufflinks for the blouse, and one or two brooches. The purse closing is made of brass or silver.

Man's bunad from Romerike

This man's bunad was re-designed after a painting that showed congressman Anders Haneborg in knickers and a long, light colored jacket. It was painted about 1810. The vest was copied after a vest from Nannestad, dated about 1830. You find the painting in the Norwegian Folk Museum. It was Åsmund Svinndal in cooperation with «Heimen», who designed the bunad in 1952.

The jacket is made of white frieze. It has a single row of buttons, a little stand-up collar and pocket flaps. The button holes are made with red colored thread, and the pocket flaps have red colored lining. It has knickers made of black wool material, and a fly in front, waist-band with a buckle, and a row of silver buttons by the knees. The vest is made of blue colored wool material with white stripes. It has a single row of buttons, and fits high up around the neckline, with a little stand-up collar. The shirt is made of white linen, with whitework around the collar and cuffs of the sleeves. White patterned stockings, and garters in a variety of colors, and black shoes with buckles are part of the bunad. The silver consists of a neck pin or a neck brooch, button cufflinks and the buttons on the jacket, the vest and the knickers.

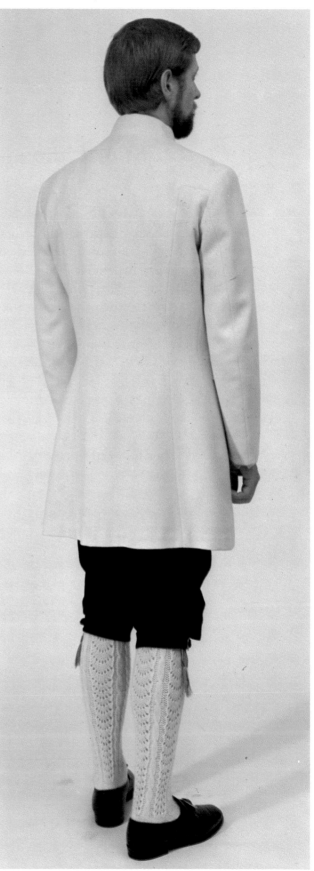

Woman's bunad from Bærum

The idea behind a bunad for Bærum, was brought to light in 1946. «Bondekvinnelaget» and «Bærum Husflidsforening» got together, and in 1963 the bunad was completed. We do not know of any folk costume traditions from Bærum, so antique clothes and fabrics from the district were used to design the bunad. The hat's design came from an old hat from Levre. The skirt is a copy of vest material from Øverland. The whitework for the blouse was copied from an embroidered vest from Ringerike.

The skirt is plaid, double shuttle-weave, half-woolen material. It is finely pleated. The bodice is made of red, hand-woven, half-woolen material. It has lacing in front. The blouse is made of white linen, with whitework and tatting around the collar and cuffs of the sleeves. The apron is made of hand-woven, eight shuttle-weave, half-woolen material in green color. It has a woven belt, with a silver buckle in front. The hat is made of black wool damask, or green colored velvet. It has a silk bow in back and can be designed with or without tie ribbons. It has white lace-work around the edge. Black shoes and black stockings are part of the bunad. We use a medium long cape for the outdoors, made of black wool material, with a lining made of red wool material. The bunad's silver consists of silver eyelets and silver chain for the bodice, a little neck brooch and a bigger brooch for the blouse. There is no silver jewelry especially made for this costume, so the silver jewelry used for this model is called Valdressilver.

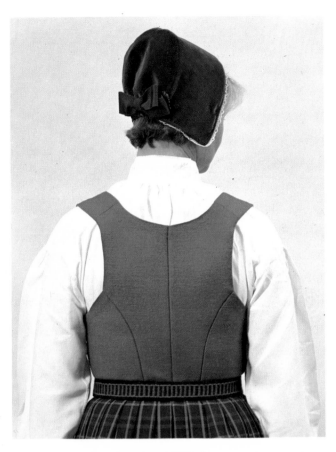

HEDMARK

The entire collection of bunads from Hedmark came as a result of the bunad movement that began in this century. The traditional man's costume had never been out of use, and it was officially named the Østerdal bunad. Hulda Garborg writes in her book «Norwegian Costumes», that the woman's bunad from Nord-Østerdal had been in use up until 1917. It used to consist of a black colored dress/jumper, a chequered blouse and a «black hat» or «honnlue». A later variation of the woman's bunad from Nord-Østerdal consisted of a green skirt, a red bodice and a silk shawl. It came into use about 1920.

When a competition to design the bunad for Nord-Østerdal was announced in 1946, many different bunads were designed, most of them were embroidered models, and with no traditional background. The most famous costumes are the Marie Åen's costume and the Løderup costume, both of which have been in use for a long time. In addition as well Kvikne, Alvdal, Tynset, Solør as Odal have their own costumes. A woman's bunad and a man's bunad were designed for both Solør and Odal in the 1950s. The woman's bunad for Sør-Østerdal was designed in the 1930s, and was later re-designed in the 1960s. The costume was copied after antique garments at the Glomdals Museum, dated about the 1700s. The antique cloths garments varied in style and colours, and that same option is also kept for the todays Sør-Østerdal bunad. The woman's bunad for Hedmark was designed in 1935, and re-designed in 1952. It was copied after a painting called «Girl from Hedmark», made by J.F.L. Dreier. Dreier painted folk costume pictures from Hedmark, mostly from Østerdalen.

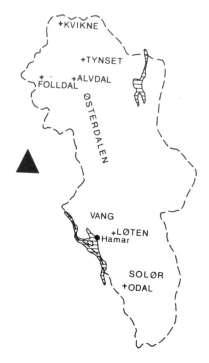

«Costumes from Tønset». From Chr. Tønsberg «Norwegian National Costumes», Christiania 1852.

Woman's bunad from Hedmark

The Hedmark bunad was designed in 1935, by «Hedmark Fylkes Husflidskomite.» The design for the bunad is shown in a painting called, «Girl from Hedemarken», painted about the last part of the 18th C. The girl in the painting has a light blue costume, and a bodice with a peplum. The bodice was designed after an old bodice from Løten, the skirt's material came from Vang. Both pieces are now on display in Hedmark Museum. The Hedmark bunad was redesigned in 1952. Instead of the plain colored bodice, a new copy of a bodice from Stange was made of silk pattern material. The antique embroidery that used to be in yellow and red colors, was changed to other colors.

The skirt is made of light blue colored, double shuttle-weave, wool material, with dark blue stripes, and small rose pattern in wool yarn. The skirt is finely pleated. The bodice can be made in light blue, red or yellow brocade/damask, and it has a peplum. It has a concealed opening in front. The blouse is made of white linen with whitework on part of the shoulders, around the high standing collar and on both sides of the neck opening and cuffs of the sleeves. The hat is made of brocade material, in a flower pattern. It has a silver lace around the edge. It is made of two matching pieces of material. The purse is made of the same material as the skirt. It has a metal closing. Grey or black stockings and black shoes are part of the costume. A cape in blue wool material is made for the outdoors. This bunad does not have any particular silver jewelry made for it. One or two brooches can be used for this bunad.

Woman's bunad from Solør and Odal

The woman's bunad from Solør and Odal was designed in 1958. Behind the idea was the district folkdance committee, «Varden». The bodice was copied from a bodice with a scalloped peplum, from Heradsbygd, in Solør, now to be found at the Glomdal Museum. The embroidery on the blouse was copied from an embroidery on a groom's shirt sleeves. The little tucked hat has the same design as the antique hats from the districts Solør and Odal.

The skirt is made of black, green or blue wool material. It is pleated with a plain center panel. The bodice is made of pattern-woven brocade, in black, beige or red, as background colors, and it has buckskin around the edges. The bodice has a schalloped peplum design. It has lacing in front that closes with a chain in silver. The blouse is made of white linen, with tatting around the collar and cuffs of the sleeves. The hat is made of silk. It has a tucked crown and a plain front piece, and it has ribbons that can be tied under the chin, or just hang loose. And it also has white lace around the edge. For the outdoors we use a scarf that is made of home-woven black wool with a fringe. Black stockings and black shoes are part of the costume. The bunad's silver consists of button cufflinks, a brooch for the blouse, and eyelets and chain for the bodice.

Man's bunad from Solør and Odal

This bunad was designed in the 1950s by the district folk dance committee, «Varden». The bunad's knickers were copied from old light colored knickers, and the jacket was copied from an antique jacket, both to be found at the Norwegian Folk Museum.

The jacket is made of black frieze. It has a row of pewter buttons on each side of the jacket's opening, and buttons on cuffs of the sleeves. It has a high standing collar and turn-down cuffs. It has knickers made of frieze with a fly in front. It has a waistband with a buckle in front and a row of pewter buttons by the knees. The vest is made of hand-woven wool material, in red, brown and black striped and checked pattern. It has double rows of pewter buttons. It has no collar, but turn-down lapels. The shirt is made of cotton cloth with tatting around the collar and cuffs of the sleeves. It has a cap with a visor. White knitted stockings with garters in a variety of colors and black bunad shoes. The bunad's jewelry consists of a neck brooch and button cufflinks for the shirt. All the buttons for the shirt, the knickers and the vest are made of pewter.

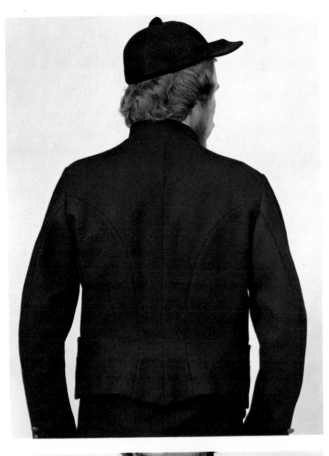

Woman's bunad from Sør-Østerdal

Elverum Husflidslag redesigned the Sør-Østerdal bunad in the 1960s. It had been in use since the 1930s. A few antique costume materials from Sør-Østerdal, from the last part of the 18th. C until the first part of the 19th C, have been preserved, now to be found at the Glomdal Museum. Some of these costumes were used as copies for the new bunad. The antique costume differs in design so they gave the new Sør-Østerdal bunad a free choice of materials and colors. The jacket we see in the photo (opposite page) is copied after a jacket found at the Glomdal Museum (the owner born in 1783). The white blouse is copied from the «Strand-shirt» (the owner born in 1719). The bunad can be used with the jacket or the bodice with the blouse under. It has a hat for women and a hat for girls. Different materials and different colors can be used to make the skirt, the bodice, the jacket, the apron, the hat and the shoulder scarf.

The skirt is made of wool damask or double shuttle weave, wool material, in the colors black, blue or green. It has a plain front panel, pleated sides and tucked-in back. The jacket is made of red or brown pattern woven, wool material. The jacket has a peplum and a concealed opening in front. The bodice is made of pattern woven wool material and it has a peplum. It can be made in blue, brown or two different red colors. The blouse is made of white linen. The blouses can be made in four different styles.

All the blouses are without collars. One of the blouses is copied after a blouse with wide sleeves, and filled double drownwork, and a basic seam around the edges. The apron is made of cotton material or mohair, with black printed pattern. (The antique aprons had woven patterns.) The apron is pleated with braided tie bands. The girl's hat has a flat crown and a plain front piece. The woman's hat has a high tucked crown. Both hats are made of silk pattern material, with bands that can be tied under the chin. The shoulder scarf is made of silk pattern material with fringes. The corners of the shoulder scarf are tucked inside the jacket or the bodice. Black stockings and black shoes are part of the costume. We use a medium long cape, in red or blue pattern woven material, for the outdoors. It has a high stand-up collar and closes around the neck with a silver buckle. One or two brooches are used for the bunad. The biggest silver brooch is heart-shaped. It looks simple, but the casting was the most difficult. The brooch has different dangles and in addition they use Danish/Norwegian royal monograms.

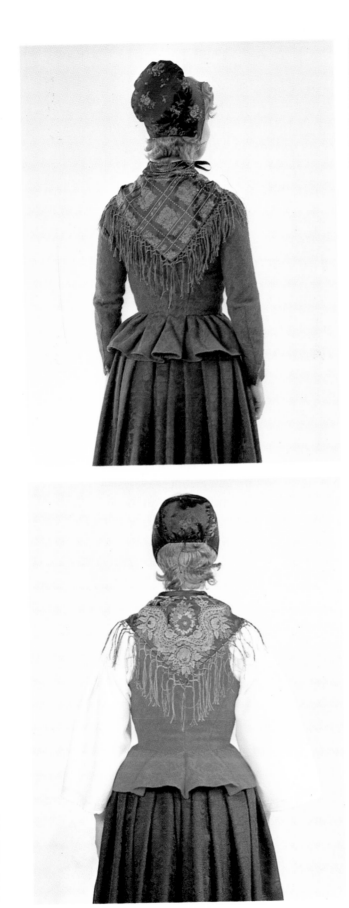

Woman's bunad from Nord-Østerdal

This bunad was in use before 1920. The bunad was designed upon traditional old bodices and skirts from the area. But there is no continuation of the bunad that was used back in Hulda Garborg's days: «Honnluen» is the same as the one Hulda Garborg described. The first years they used scarves called, «kløvgang» or «lynild». But when they quit making these black silk scarves, «Den Norske Husflidsforening» in Oslo designed a new black silk scarf with stripes that is called the Nord-Østerdal-scarf.

The skirt is made of green colored wool damask. It is pleated with a straight front panel, and a tucked part in back. The bodice is made of red colored damask. It joins in front with a concealed closing. The blouse is made of white linen, with whitework around the high standing collar and cuffs of the sleeves. The apron is made of red, black and green checked pattern in wool material. The hat is a «honnlue» made of the same material as the bodice, or black silk. It has white lace around the edge, and a ribbon that can be tied under the chin. Black stockings and black shoes are part of the costume. Østerdalen has it's own designed bunad-silver. The brooch that closes the collar was designed in Nord-Østerdal.

Man's bunad from Østerdalen

As a folk costume, the short fitted jacket and knickers were in use in Østerdalen in the last part of the 19th C. As early as 1905, the man's bunad was photographed. The vest used to be black, but the new design has a checked vest.

The jacket is made of black frieze. It has a row of silver buttons on each side of the opening in front. It can't be buttoned. It has a little stand-up collar but no cuffs. The knickers are made of black colored frieze material. It has a waistband and a buckle in front, and a row of buttons by the knees. It has a fly. The vest is made of red and black checked material. It also has two rows of silver buttons in front. It has a little stand-up collar and turn-back lapels which close with a silver button on each sleeve. The shirt is made of cotton cloth. A cap with a visor is part of the bunad. The stockings are knitted in solid white or in a black and white pattern. The garters are made in a variety of colors that are tied under the cuffs of the knickers. Only the tassels can be seen. Black shoes with buckles are part of the bunad. The bunad's silver consists of all the silver buttons on the jacket, the vest and the knickers. They can also be made of pewter. The shirt closes around the neckline with a little silver pin.

OPPLAND

«**R**ondastakken» is the only bunad in Oppland that is a direct continuation of the original folk costume. There are quite a few embroidered costumes from Gudbrandsdalen, copied from antique, embroidered skirts and bodices from the last part of the 18th and 19th century. Large plaid material came into fashion in the last century. Later it came back into fashion, and was used for the woman's bunad from Lesja and Gausdal.

The Gudbrandsdal man's bunad of today is copied from a recent design. It consists of a short dark colored jacket and a pair of trousers. A re-design of the «Grey vest costume» is in progress. It was in use about the 1700s and first half of the last century. It has a knee-length grey vest, with pleats in back and large decorated pocket-flaps. Hulda Garborg used her own ideas to design the woman's bunad from Valdres. She designed an embroidered costume for Valdres in 1914. The antique folk costume had then been out of use for a long time. Antique formal costumes were in use in different areas, but the people from the area prefered the embroidered costume instead of the traditional one. The Valdres bunad was re-designed in the 1940s, and the result was an embroidered model completed in 1948 that was used in addition to the original costume. With help from Johannes Flintoes costume paintings and preserved antique costume material, a woman's bunad for Vang and Slidre was re-designed in the 1970s. A plain checkered jumper/dress type of costume was used in Valdres well into this century. The traditional «Rutastakken» is a popular costume today. The man's bunad from Valdres is copied from the most recent folk costume which was in use in the last part of the 19th C. It consisted of a short dark-colored jacket and trousers. Some men used an embroidered costume, with a ¾ length jacket and embroidered knickers. Hallingdal used the same costume. It was copied after men's bunads from the first part of the 19th C, found in paintings by Johannes Flintoe. The woman's bunad for Land and Hadeland was designed in 1927. The Hadeland bunad did not become popular. Vest-Oppland got it's bunad in 1939.

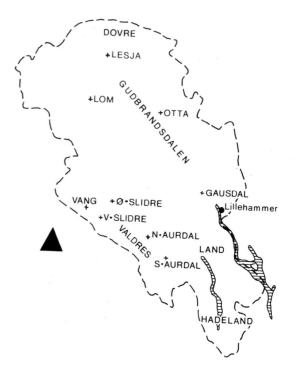

«Women in Ronda costume», Lom ca. 1885. Photo: Wilse (Norwegian Folk Museum).

Woman's bunad from Gudbrandsdalen: «Rondastakken»

We find only one continuation of the folk costume tradition in Gudbrandsdalen, the «Rondastakken». The name, «rondastakk», stems from the stripes, «rondene», in the skirt's material. We can see from old skirts that there were many ways to «ronde». It means different ways to design stripes. When we compare the old bunad, from the last century, with the bunad we use today, we find that the bodice is designed longer now and the skirt is shorter. And the striped pattern skirt material does not have as many variations as it used to have in the old days.

The skirt is made of double shuttle weave, wool material. It is pleated and has an extra hem that conceals a joining of the skirt's material. The bodice is made of checked wool material. It is fastened to the skirt. It is cut straight around the waistline, and closes in front with concealed hooks. The jacket is made of dark, wool material. It is short with wide tucked sleeves. It closes in front at the waistline and around the neckline with concealed hooks. The blouse is made of white linen or cotton material with tatting, «hålagge» or «musagge», around the collar and cuffs of the sleeves. The apron is made of half-woolen material, with horizontal stripes. The kerchief is called «stiva-turklæ», it is made of white, starched linen or cotton material. It has tatting around the edge. It is very important that the «stivaturklæet» (kerchief) has the right amount of starch in it. The way the kerchief is folded gives it a triangular shape in back. Black stockings and black shoes are part of the costume. The silver consists of one or two brooches, and button cufflinks for the blouse.

50

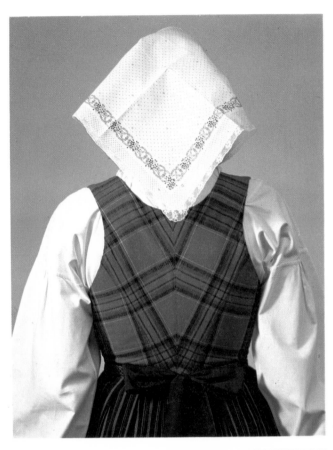

Woman's bunad from Gudbrandsdalen «Grafferbunaden»

A few solid-colored wool skirts with flower pattern embroidery from Gudbrandsdalen have been preserved. Some of them are from the 18th C, they look a lot like the embroidered dresses and skirts that were customary in the cities around the 18th C. This bunad was copied from a city-styled dress, it came from Graffer in Lom. We don't know what the bodice was like. The Graffer-bunad was redesigned in the 1950s. Before that they had used a poor copy with a different bodice. The new Graffer-bunad has a straight waistline, attached to the skirt, like the original design from Gudbrandsdalen, from about the 1830s. The Graffer-bunad became very popular, and it became a model for other embroidered bunads in other parts of the country.

The skirt is made of blue wool material with embroidery in a variety of colors, in metallic thread and woolen yarn. The skirt is pleated with a kick-pleat in back. The bodice is made of red colored linen damask. It has a straight waistline and is attached to the skirt. It closes in front with four or five concealed hooks, from the waistline up. The jacket is fitted to the body, it is made of blue colored wool material. It has wide tucked sleeves, and closes in front with concealed hooks and a silver buckle on the collar. The blouse is made of white linen or cotton cloth, it has a turn-down collar. The hat is made of the same material as the skirt, and it has flower pattern embroidery on both sides and in back. The purse is made of wool material and has the same flower pattern embroidery. The purse closing is made of silver or brass. Black stockings and black shoes are part of the costume. The silver consists of two brooches and button cufflinks for the blouse. They use the bigger brooch higher up on the blouse and the smaller one below.

The formal costume from Gudbrandsdalen

Anna and Aksel Johannessen from Lillehammer designed this costume in the 1920s. The flower pattern embroidery was copied from an antique, blue-green colored skirt, with a flower pattern in a variety of colors, now to be found at the Norwegian Folk Museum. The antique costume had a solid-colored bodice attached to the skirt. Aksel Johannessen transferred the same flower pattern that is on the skirt to the bodice, the hat and later to the apron. There have been a variety of flower pattern-embroidered bunads from Gudbrandsdalen since the last part of the 18th C. About 1830, it was common to see a short bodice, attached to the skirt. We know of solid-colored and flower pattern-embroidered bodices from the district. None of the antique costumes had flower pattern embroidery on the skirt and bodice. The apron is not so common in Gudbrandsdalen as in other parts of the country.

Today this bunad is made in blue, black or white colors. It can be used with or without an apron. The skirt is made of solid-colored wool material, with flower pattern embroidery in a variety of colors. It is loosely pleated. The bodice is made of the same material as the skirt, and it has the same flower pattern embroidery in both back and front. The bodice is short and is attached to the skirt. It has a concealed closing in front, but does not close all the way up. The blouse is made of white linen or cotton cloth, it has tatting on the turn-down collar and cuffs of the sleeves. The apron is made of the same material as the skirt, and it has the same embroidery as the skirt's border embroidery. The bunad can be used with or without apron. The hat is made of the same material as the rest of the costume. It has embroidery both in front and in back. Black stockings and black shoes with buckles are part of the costume. The silver consists of two brooches and button cufflinks for the blouse.

Woman's bunad from Gudbrandsdalen

This bunad and the formal costume «Gudbrandsdalens festbunad» from the preceeding page, both have the same model. The skirt was originally made in blue color, and the bodice was made in solid, red colored damask. «Husfliden» in Oslo designed this bunad in the beginning of the 1950s.

The skirt is made of blue, wool material, with a thin red border stripe. It has a rose pattern made of metallic thread and woolen yarn, made in a variety of colors. The skirt is pleated and it has a concealed pocket on one side. The bodice is made of red colored linen damask. It closes in front with concealed hooks, a little higher than the waistline. The blouse is made of white linen, with whitework and tatting around the turn-down collar and cuffs of the sleeves, and whitework on part of the shoulders. The hat is made of black or blue silk. It has a tucked crown and a plain front piece, with a red colored silk band and white lace around the front edge. It has a ribbon that can be tied under the chin. Black stockings and black shoes are part of the costume. The bunad's silver consists of one or two brooches and button cufflinks.

Woman's bunad from Lesja

They started working on the idea for the Lesja bunad in the 1920s. Helga Doseth was in charge. A few large antique, vegetable-dyed, plaid pattern materials from Lesja were preserved. And these were used as copy for the new costume. Striped and plaid wool materials like these were in use around the 19th C. The bunad has a dress/jumper design, that was customary in Gudbrandsdalen, from the last part of the 18th C. They used kerchiefs in all parts of Gudbrandsdalen called «stivaturkle». Many antique blouses from Lesja were preserved. The bunad's blouse was copied after a blouse that belonged to Åse Hauje. Her bridal costume from 1812 was among some of the different costumes she made.

This costume is designed like a dress/jumper, with the bodice attached to the skirt. The material is vegetable-dyed, double shuttle weave, all-wool with plaid-woven pattern material. Different patterns can also be embroidered on the plaid material. The skirt is pleated, with a kick-pleat in the back. The bodice ends a little above the waistline. It closes with concealed hooks in front. The blouse is made of white linen or cotton cloth, with whitework around the high standing collar, and cuffs of the sleeves. It can be used with or without apron. The kerchief, «stivaturkleet» is made of thin white material, with lace around the edges. It is important that the kerchief be straight in back. A shawl is used for the outdoors. White, red or black stockings and black shoes are part of the costume. The bunad silver consists of a big brooch with dangles. Lesja has silversmith traditions and the big brooch on this model is a copy of an antique Lesja brooch.

Two men's bunads from Gudbrandsdalen

These two men's bunads were copied from later designed folk costumes that were in use in the latter part of the last century, and in some places also in this century. But from the 18th C, we know of another man's bunad from Gudbrandsdalen. It had tight fitted knickers, made of buckskin, and a long oblique designed vest. They used to wear a long, greyish jacket with large pocket flaps with edging around and large buttons. It was tucked in the back. This is the design we recognize from old photographs.

Man's bunad I (left)

The jacket is copied after an old jacket from Vågå. It is made of black wool material, with two rows of silver buttons in front. It cannot be buttoned. It has a stand-up collar and turn-down cuffs. The jacket has a straight seam in the middle and two oblique seams. It has knickers made of wool material. It has a fly, and a row of silver buttons by the knee. The vest can be made of brocade, like the one in the photo, or it can be made of checked wool material. It has a row of silver buttons on each side of the opening in front, and it has turn-back lapels. The shirt is made of cotton cloth with tatting around the collar and cuffs of the sleeves. White knitted stockings and garters made in a variety of colors, and black shoes with buckles, are part of the costume. The bunad silver consists of neck buttons or a neck brooch, button cufflinks and all the silver buttons for the jacket, the knickers and the vest.

Man's bunad II (right)

This man's bunad was copied from a man's costume from Skjåk, now to be found in the Maihaugen Museum. It was originally designed as a bunad by a tailor from Vinstra in 1965. The jacket is made of black cloth, decorated with stitches. It has two rows of silver buttons, one on each side of the front opening. It has a stand-up collar and turn-down cuffs. The jacket has a straight seam in the middle, and two oblique seams. The knickers are made of the same material as the jacket, and with a fly. The vest is made of brocade material. It has a single row of buttons in front, and turn-back lapels. The shirt is made of cotton cloth, and it has tatting around the collar and cuffs of the sleeves. Black shoes with buckles are part of the costume. The bunad silver consists of a neck pin, button cufflinks for the shirt, and the buttons for the jacket and vest.

Woman's bunad from Vang and Slidre

This bunad was redesigned in 1971. It is copied from an antique costume from the 19th C and a Johannes Flintoe painting called «The Housewife in a Formal Costume», painted about 1820. A few antique costumes from Valdres have been preserved. The jacket is copied after a «føldetrøye» jacket found at Valdres Folk Museum. The copies for the blouse, a short blouse, (trøyelekkja), the chain and buckle on the jacket and the button cufflinks are also found at Valdres Folk Museum. The belt and the bodice insert are copied after a belt and bodice insert from Beito. The copy for the woman's hat, «rullen», comes from Lykkja in Øystre Slidre. In Flintoes' paintings these women's hats are used with the formal costumes, and a blue hat is used with the daily costume. Young girls wear their hair loose or in a ponytail with bands around. But for formal occasions, they braid their hair with bands in plaits. They also wear a silk scarf around the head, in front of the braids.

The original costume was in use from the last part of the 18th C up until about 1850—1860.

The skirt is made of finely pleated black wool material. The jacket is made of red colored frieze with green silk edging. It is called a «føldetrøye» and it has a pleated peplum. The jacket is open in front, with a loose insert. The bodice is made of red wool damask, with black velvet around the edges. It is open in front with a loose insert. The insert is made of red wool material with embroidery in a variety of colors. The trim is made of black velvet. The blouse is made of white linen with whitework around the collar and cuffs of the sleeves. A shorter blouse is used instead of the regular length blouse. The apron is made of white cotton material with printed flower patterns. It is hard to get the same quality printed materials as they used for the antique aprons. The belt is made of red wool material, with the same kind of embroidery as the insert. The hat is made for married women, and is called «rull». It is made of red colored frieze material, and is round in shape. A white crochet snood is pulled over the hat.

A folded scarf in a variety of colors is tied around the head with a bow in front. A neck scarf, also in a variety of colors, is to be worn outside the collar and tied in a bow. Blue or black stockings and black shoes are part of the costume. The bunad silver consists of two brooches and button cufflinks for the blouse and button cufflinks, buckle and chain for the jacket.

Woman's bunad from Valdres — «Rutastakken»

«Rutastakken» (checked costume) is copied from an antique dress/jumper from Semeleng in Vestre Slidre, where it was in use in the 1840s. These checked costumes were worn until the beginning of this century. Many home woven wool materials, in different checked patterns were made in various districts of Valdres. The material used for this model is called «sumelengji-material», copied from the original bunad from Semeleng. Only one out of several «checked material» is used for this particular bunad.

The skirt is made of home woven, checked, wool material. The pattern can vary some. The skirt is pleated in front and tucked in back. The bodice is made of the same material as the skirt, and is attached to the skirt. It closes in front with concealed hooks. The blouse is made of white linen or cotton cloth, with whitework around the collar and cuffs of the sleeves. The apron is made of home woven, half-woolen material and it has a horizontal striped pattern, with bands that can be tied in a bow in the back. The hat can be made of velvet or other appropriate material. In the photo, we can see a hat designed in a silk damask pattern. Black stockings and shoes are part of the costume. The silver consists of two brooches and button cufflinks for the blouse. Valdres has its own designs of bunad silver, that builds upon old traditions.

Woman's bunad from Valdres

The woman's bunad from Valdres was designed in 1914, with the help of Hulda Garborg. The traditional custumes had not been in use for quite a few years. The familiar formal costume was not fitted as a bunad. So they designed a new Valdres bunad, a dress/jumper design, with embroidery copied from a hat and a scarf. A redesign in 1948 changed the Valdres bunad. It was copied after a checked model from Semeleng, (the same model that was used for the «checked costume»). The embroidery was copied from a different velvet hat. The «new Valdres bunad» was finished in 1948. (Photo on next page)

The bunad can be made in grey-blue or black colors. The skirt is made of grey-blue or black wool material; it has embroidery around the border, designed in a variety of colors. The skirt it pleated in front and tucked in back. The bodice is made of the same material as the skirt and is attached to the skirt. The bodice has wool yarn embroideries on both sides of the front opening and in back. It closes in front with concealed hooks. The blouse is made of white linen, with whitework around the collar and cuffs of the sleeves. The hat is made of the same material as the rest of the bunad, and it has the same wool yarn embroideries, both in front and in back. The purse has the same embroidery and is made of the same material. The purse closing is made of silver or brass. The silver consists of button cufflinks and two brooches. Valdres has old silversmith traditions and the silver used for this model is called Valdres silver.

Man's bunad from Valdres

The short designed jacket from the 1800s came back into fashion for men in Valdres. Today's design is copied from a short jacket from Garli in Nord-Aurdal, and the knickers, with a flap, from Sør-Aurdal. The vest is copied after different antique vests. The Valdres Bunad Committee designed it in 1962. Bunads like the one in the photograph (opposite page) had been in use for years.

The jacket is made of black wool material, with black velvet edges. It has a stand-up collar and turn-back lapels, and a row of silver buttons on each side of the opening in front and on cuffs of the sleeves. It cannot be buttoned. The trousers are made of the same material as the jacket. Either knickers or trousers can be used. The knickers have a waistband with a buckle in front, and a row of silver buttons by the knees. They have a flap. The vest is made of home-woven, checked wool material. The checked patterns can differ. For this model they used a copy of antique skirt material, from Semeleng in Vestre Slidre. It has two rows of silver buttons, stand-up collar, and turn-back lapels. The shirt is made of white linen or cotton cloth, with tatting around the collar and cuffs of the sleeves. And a colored neck cloth can be worn outside the shirt collar. Knitted stockings in white or blue and white pattern and black shoes with buckles are part of the costume. Garters in a variety of colors are used with the knickers. The bunad's silver consists of neck button, button cufflinks and silver buttons for the jacket, vest and trousers.

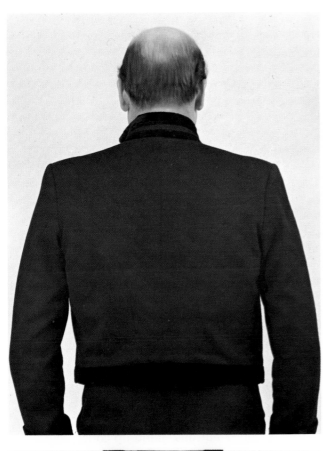

BUSKERUD

Folk costumes from Hallingdal were not an unusual sight in the streets of Hønefoss in the 1950s. And older women from Flesberg wore their bunads on shopping trips up until the 1960s. Hallingdal and Numedal in Buskerud are among the places where the folk costumes have been in fashion the longest, and authenticity of the costumes has been proven.

There has been a difference in the traditional costumes from Upper Numedal and Flesberg, since about the 1800s. They distinguish between the woman's bunad from Upper Hallingdal, in Ål parish, Gol, Nes and Flå. In the second part of last century, women from Flå used a different costume than was used in the rest of Hallingdal. This costume had a «sjart», meaning: the jacket has a stiffened edge. This woman's costume was also used in Krødsherad, Sigdal, Eggedal and Upper Numedal. (Old pictures and costumes from those areas indicate that). Sigdal got a new woman's bunad in the 1930s, which is also used in Krødsherad. The Sigdal bunad is being re-designed. The valley area has a different costume than the rest of the district. It has been difficult to find any folk costume traditions at all among the residents of the flatland. They started to work on a new bunad for Ringerike in 1935; it was copied from antique costume material and a painting, made by Ådnes, at the Ringerike Museum. A re-design was begun in the 1950s, but is not completed yet. In the meantime, another bunad was designed for Ringerike. It has a flower-embroidered jumper/dress, without any traditional background. Eiker got it's own bunad, which became the bunad for the entire lower part of Buskerud. The flower embroidery, designed by Halfdan Arneberg, also has no traditional background.

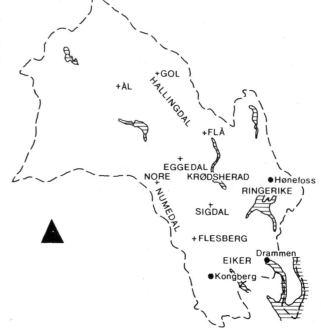

«Porridge women». Painting by Theodor Kittelsen from Sigdal, 1904. (From an old postcard. University Library).

Woman's bunad from Flesberg

The woman's bunad from Flesberg was in daily use up until 1950—1960. The Flesberg bunad is an exact replica of the traditional folk costume. It was in use in the beginning of the 19th C. At the same time, the «skjælings-kleda» became formal costume in upper Numedal. From then on the costumes in the upper and lower Numedal were different in design. Decorative bands are used for both bodice and jacket, the aprons and scarves have varied, but they always had a simple design depending on what kind of material and band one could get. The bunad from Flesberg has more than one skirt in use at the same time. As many as seven skirts have been used at one time. But in recent years, two or three were more customary, when the costume was in traditional use. In the photographs we see two versions of the bunad, a younger and an older model. The photo on the opposite page shows the older model, with a black hacket. Next page shows the younger version of the bunad, with «nyvevnadtrøya», the new jacket. Both are being used at the present.

The shirt is made of black wool material, with a green border stripe. It is finely pleated and more than one skirt should be used. «Nestutapåstakken», the second skirt, is made in green, with a red border stripe. The Flesberg bunad should be bulky. The skirt has wide embroidered suspenders. A little piece of the suspenders should be visible on the shoulders, between the skirt and jacket. They are fastened to the «Nestutapåstakken», skirt number two.

The jacket is made of black wool material, with decorative lilac bands around the edges. The jacket shown in the photos is an heirloom but still in use. It has lilac velvet bands but they are no longer in stock. It closes in front with concealed hooks. The bodice is made of black wool material, and it has the same decorative bands as the jacket. It has a little split in front, to show off the blouse. The bodice has a half circle of silver buttons on each side in front; when buttoned, it forms a circle. Only the upper and lower buttons can be buttoned. The blouse is made of white linen, with whitework or colored embroidery in wool yarn around cuffs of the sleeves. The collar can be with or without embroidery. The apron is made of black wool with printed flower pattern, in a variety of colors. The hat can be used with or without a scarf around. The head scarf goes twice around the head, and is tied in a bow in front. The head scarf has a hat underneath, that is made of patterned silk material in back and cotton in front. The hat is used separately and is then made of silk material. Both hats fit over the ears and have wide bands that can be tied under the chin. A patterned neck scarf of silk tied in a bow is used. Dark blue patterned stockings, or black stockings and black shoes, are part of the costume. A medium length cape is used for the outdoors. The bunad silver consists of a costume ring, a brooch, and button cufflinks for the blouse; silver buttons for the bodice and button cufflinks for the jacket.

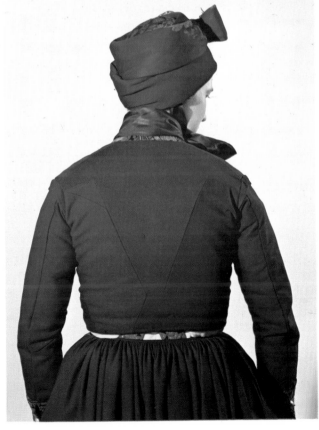

Woman's bunad from Flesberg «nyvevnadtrøye»

This version of the Flesberg bunad, «nyvevnadtrøye», has been in use for most of this century. The only difference from the older model is the jacket.

The most recently designed jacket has wide sleeves and a high standing collar, and it is used under the bodice. The older model has a black jacket with narrow sleeves. Both bunads can be used for formal and daily purposes. In the 1880s, the women from Flesberg were taught how to weave «nyvevnad», a rotating technique in black with pattern in red and green. The jackets were used for formal occasions. When they started to use the new jacket, they quit using the forehead scarf over the cap and the apron with the skirt.

The skirt is made of black wool material and it has a green border stripe. It is finely pleated, and more than one skirt is used at the same time. «Nestutapå-stakken», the second skirt, is in green with a red border stripe. It has wide embroidered suspenders. The jacket, «nyvevnadtrøya», is made of red and black striped home-woven material, with wool and cotton mixed. It has wide sleeves with cuffs, and short, stand-up collar. It closes in front with a row of silver buttons. For formal occasions, the bodice is used over the jacket. The bodice is made of black wool material with velvet edging. It has a split in front, to show off part of the jacket and its buttons. The bodice has a half circle of silver buttons on each side in front; when buttoned they form a circle. Only the upper and lower buttons can be buttoned. A neck scarf made of wool or silk is tied in a bow. The hat is made of silk, with velvet bands by the ears. And with wide silk bands that can be tied under the chin. Black stockings and black shoes are part of the costume. The bunad silver consists of a brooch and the buttons on the «nyvevnadstrøya», the jacket, and the silver buttons on the bodice.

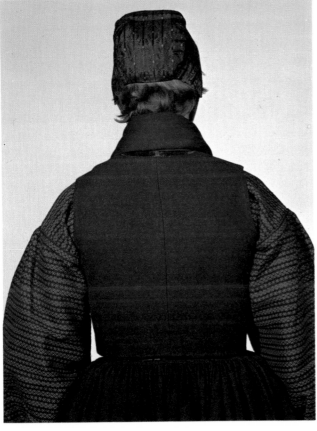

Man's bunad from Flesberg

This man's bunad from Flesberg is exactly like the one that was in use from the first part of the 19th C. It has knickers, vest, and a half-length jacket, «gråtrøya». Many antique costumes and pictures from Numedal are preserved. They show the way the people dressed in the old days. This costume was used up until the mid 19th C. Then it was changed to the dark-colored, shorter, tight-fitting designed jacket, called «rundtrøye-kleda». It was in use in many parts of the country. In the early 20th C the men from Flesberg stopped wearing bunad. The city-style took over. It came back in style again in Kongsberg, however, in the 1920s and 1930s, in connection with folk dance.

It has a half-length jacket called «gråtrøya», made of white frieze, with edges in red and green. It has wedge-shaped inserts in the back and on the shoulders. It has a little, stand-up collar, and the front edges on each side of the opening are turned back. It cannot be buttoned. The knickers are made of black frieze with red embroidery and red colored button-holes. It has cuffs with buckles and a row of buttons made of silver or brass by the knees. It has a flap in front with a large brass button on each side.

The vest is made of green wool material with red-stitched button holes. It has a row of silver buttons on each side in front. The shirt is made of white linen with embroidery on the collar and cuffs of the sleeves. The embroidery can be made in white or in colors. A colored neck scarf can be tied in a bow in front.

The hat is made of green velvet with green silk bands and a tassel and an edge of otter or beaver skin. White patterned knitted stockings and black shoes are part of the costume. The bunad silver consists of a neck button for the shirt, and silver buttons for the bodice. Antique button patterns from Numedal were used to copy the buttons for the new bunad.

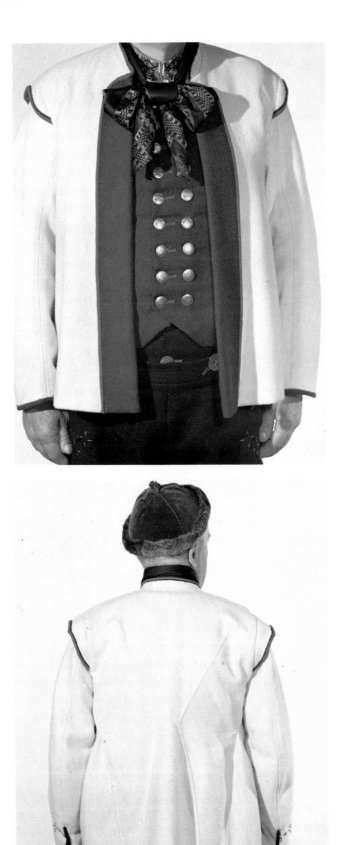

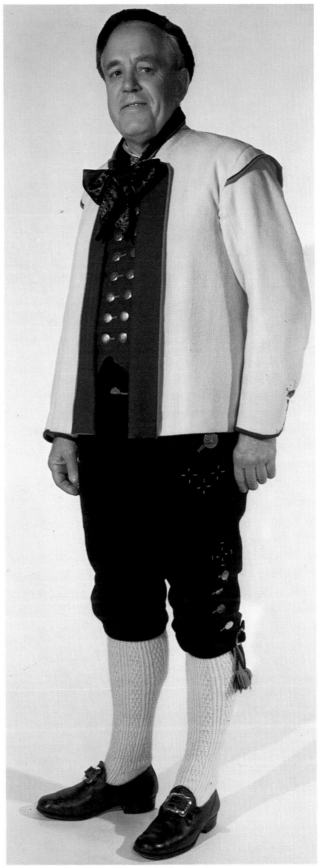

Woman's bunad from Øvre Numedal

This bunad is a copy of the «skjælingskleda» that were in use in Øvre Numedal in the early 19th C. The name, «skjælingskleda» means that the edges, both on the bodice and the jacket, are stiffened. They are called «skjæling». These costumes were expensive, and were made by a tailor. They stopped using «skjælingskleda» as a formal costume around 1900. Old costumes are preserved, and some have been used as bunads in this century. The antique costumes show that there were variations in colors, materials, and decoration bands. The «skjælingstrøya», (the jacket) has always been in black, but the bodice and the skirt can be made in both blue and black colors. The bands around the edges used to be brown, black or in velvet flower-patterns. It is not possible to get bands like that today, so they use a woven silk band that looks a lot like the old velvet bands. They used a lot of different materials for the apron in the last century, both solid-colored and patterned materials of silk and fine wool. There was little difference between the costumes from upper and lower Numedal before the time of the «skjælingskleda».

The jacket is made of black material, with black velvet bands and patterned silk bands. It is called «skjælingstrøya» because of the stiff edges, called «skjælingen». The jacket is open in front with concealed hooks. Inside the jacket, there is a loose embroidered insert. It is outside the bodice. The skirt is made of black wool material. It has a patterned silk band over the black, velvet hem. More than one skirt is customary. The skirt is finely pleated with woven or embroidered suspenders. They are fastened in back to hold the skirt up. The suspenders and part of the blouse should be visible between the skirt and the jacket. The bodice is made of the same material as the jacket, and it has the same silk bands around the edges. It has «skjæling», stiffened edge, just like the jacket. It has a short bodice, with two rows of buttons in front. Only the upper and lower buttons can be buttoned. It has a little opening in front. The insert is embroidered. Recently, beaded inserts have been used. The model in the photo shows a bunad with an antique beaded insert and silver lace. The blouse is made of white linen with whitework around the collar and cuffs of the sleeves. The embroidery can be in colors, or whitework. The apron is made of black silk with horizontal and vertical stripes. It has a woven sash, and is supposed to be wrapped around the waistline twice and hung down at one side in front. The hat has a tucked piece in back and a plain front piece. It is made of patterned silk material and has bands that can be tied under the chin. The hat is partly covered by a silk scarf that is tied in a bow. Black stockings and black shoes are part of the costume. The bunad silver consists of a neck brooch, button cufflinks for the blouse, silver buttons on the vest and on the jacket. The buttons are copied from old buttons from Øvre Numedal.

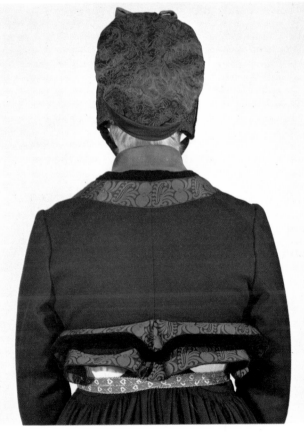

Man's bunad from Krødsherad

The folk dance group «Kryllingringen» from Krødsherad, started to use the man's bunad in the 1970s. The knickers, vest and shirt were copied after antique costumes from Sigdal, Eggedal and Krødsherad, dated about 1830. The man's bunad has a medium-length jacket, and wedge-shaped inserts in back. This jacket was called «fiskekjælke», and this jacket design was used for the new bunad.

The jacket is made of black frieze, with black velvet edges. It has wedge-shaped insets in back and these are held together on the inside of the jacket with tread loops. The jacket has a stand-up collar but no lapels. It has a row of silver buttons on each side of the opening but it cannot be buttoned. It has shoulder edges of black velvet.

The knickers are made of black frieze with a wide flap in front. They have cuffs with a row of silver buttons on the outside of the knees. Trousers can also be used. The vest is made of black wool material. It has a row of silver buttons on each side of the opening and it has turn-back lapels. The shirt is made of white linen with tatting on the cuffs of the sleeves.

A patterned silk scarf is used over the collar. The hat is made of red colored plush decorated with black velvet bands. White knitted stockings and black shoes are part of the costume. The bunad silver consists of a neck button or a ring-shaped neck pin, and all the silver buttons for the bodice, the vest and the knickers.

Woman's bunad from Øvre Hallingdal

The woman's bunad has been in traditional use up until today in Ål in Øvre Hallingdal. But the bunad design has changed. There was a special costume for church and different ones for various other occasions. Married and unmarried women had different kinds of hats. For formal occasions the «hood» for married women is still in use, but the linen headscarf for girls is no longer in use. The hat we see in the photos is much in use today. The wool yarn embroidery on the skirt became fashionable in Ål in the last part of the 19th C. Before that, they used to sew bands on the skirt and on the bodice. The bodice could be made of damask or wool material. In the last century, they used a loose insert. Many had beaded patterns. The bunad we use today is a copy of the traditional costume.

The skirt is made of black wool material with an embroidered hem in a variety of colors. The skirt is pleated and attached to the bodice. The bodice is also made of black wool, it is almost covered with wool yarn embroidery in a variety of colors. There is a silver buckle on each side of the straps connected with a chain. The blouse is made of white cotton cloth with whitework around the collar and cuffs of the sleeves. A patterned silk neck scarf is tied around the collar. The apron is made of black wool damask and it has the same embroidery as the skirt around the border-hem, and the embroidered ties. The antique costumes used to have different kinds of embroidery.

The married women from Hallingdal use a traditional hood. The headdress has a half-circle design, made of linen with embroidery. (Their hair was braided and put up in a loop.) Over this they wore a colored silk scarf with a stiff underpad, formed to the head, (it is called «the fortune scarf»). It has a long yarn tassel made in a variety of colors, and is called, «skuven». A hat made of black wool with embroidery is used by many. Black stockings and black shoes are part of the costume. The bunad silver consists of a brooch and button cufflinks for the blouse. Two silver buckles, one on each side of the bodice, are connected with a chain.

Woman's bunad from Gol and Hemsedal

The difference between the women's costumes of Gol and Hemsedal and those of upper Hallingdal in the last century was seen in the skirt, the hat and the shape of the apron. The women from Gol used a little cap instead of the «hood». For the church costume, they used a flower-patterned, muslin apron. Many girls receive a white apron as a wedding gift. Plaid aprons were used with a simply designed bunad of a wool material. The bunad from Gol had a short bodice but not as short as the one from upper Hallingdal. In the last part of the 19th C, the bodice used to be made of damask or wool material with patterned silk bands. The traditional costume from Gol was almost out of use around the turn of the century. But around 1900, Hulda Garborg redesigned the woman's bunad from Gol. A photo of Hulda Garborg with the Gol bunad can be seen in this book. Many women who use the «Hulda Garborg model» believe it is the original Gol costume. The embroideries are copied after antique costumes, which means that different antique embroideries still live on today.

The skirt is made of double shuttle weave wool damask material, with embroidery around the hem. The embroidery is made of wool yarn in a variety of colors. The skirt is pleated. The bodice is made of black cloth with wool embroidery in a variety of colors. The pattern is marked on.

It has a «hengjelekkje», a large decorative buckle connected with a silver chain. It was actually used as a closing for the jacket but it has been moved to the bodice, where it serves as a decoration. The blouse is made of white linen with whitework around the collar and cuffs of the sleeves. The apron is made of flower-patterned wool material. A plaid wool apron can also be used. The apron is pleated with wide, wool embroidered bands and red ties. Black stockings and black shoes are part of the costume.

The bunad silver consists of button cufflinks and a brooch for the blouse, and a silver buckle with a chain for the bodice. The silver is copied from antique bunad silver from Hallingdal. The silver is oxidized.

Woman's bunad from Flå

This bunad is patterned after the woman's costume that was in use in Flå in the last part of the 19th C. As in Krødsherad, Sigdal, Eggedal and upper Numedal, «skjælingskleda», or «sjarte-trøya», was in fashion in Flå. This costume got its name from the stiffened edge.

The woman's bunad from Flå was quite different in style from the other halling bunads. The bunad tradition disappeared first in the lower part of the valley. But many antique costumes from different parts of the valley are preserved. This bunad came back in use again in the 1960s. It is copied after antique costumes from Flå. The border embroidery was copied after an antique skirt dated about 1840. The embroideries may vary. The antique skirts had different embroideries. The hat used to be made of silk and it had a scarf wrapped around it, and was tied in a bow in front. The new hat is made of the same material and has the same embroidery as the skirt.

The skirt is made of wool material with wool yarn embroidery above the hem. The skirt is pleated and is attached to the bodice. The bodice is made of red silk damask, with a silver or gold lace around the edge. It has a stiffened edge, called «sjart».

The blouse is made of white linen with whitework around the collar and cuffs of the sleeves. The blouse may also have embroidery in black or in a variety of colors. The apron is made of wool material, in black background color with rose patterns, or it can be made of home-woven plaid material. The hat is made of black wool material with red edges and wool yarn embroidery in a variety of colors. It has red bands that can be tied under the chin. Black stockings and black shoes are part of the costume. The bunad silver we see in the photograph is silver heirlooms.

Man's bunad from Hallingdal

From the first part of the 19th C, a man's bunad with medium-long white, frieze jacket, with embroidery, vest and embroidered knickers was in use all over Hallingdal. About 1820, Johannes Flintoe painted men from both Hallingdal and Valdres in this costume. Many antique costumes and photographes are preserved. Thus we know that there were variations in colors and embroideries. In «Norsk Klædebunad», from 1917, Hulda Garborg wrote that men's bunads from Hallingdal had been out of use but came back in fashion in her time, as a formal costume. Today it is primarily used in Hallingdal, bud also in some parts of Valdres.

The jacket is made of white frieze, with green edges around the front opening, black cuffs of the sleeves with red edges. It has wool yarn embroideries in a variety of colors. The jacket has wedge-shaped insert in back and a stand-up collar and shoulder edgings. It cannot be buttoned. The knickers are made of black wool with wool yarn embroideries in a variety of colors. It has a flap in front, and cuffs with a buckle and a row of silver buttons by each knee. The vest is made of red wool material with black velvet edges. It has a stand-up collar and turn-back lapels, three rows of silver buttons and a silver button on each pocket. The shirt is made of white linen with whitework around the collar and cuffs of the sleeves. A patterned neck scarf in silk is worn over the collar. A little round hat in red wool material with black edges is used for this bunad. White-patterned knitted stockings and black shoes with buckles are part of the costume. The bunad silver consists of a neck button, button cufflinks and all the silver buttons for the vest and the knickers. The photo shows a pair of beaded embroidered loose cuffs from 1902.

Man's bunad from Hallingdal

This man's bunad was designed in the last part of the 19th C and is similar to the design of today. In the first part of the 19th C the bunad had knickers and «under-shirt», a vest and a medium-length jacket with wedge-shaped insert in back. In 1850 the bunad was redesigned. Then it had a short jacket, but since then it has remained the same.

The jacket is made of black cloth or a wool material with velvet bands around the edges. It has a turn-down collar and turn-back lapels. It has a row of silver buttons on each side of the opening in front. Both knickers and trousers, «langbrok», can be used. It is made of the same material as the jacket, and with a flap in front. The knickers have cuffs with a row of silver buttons by the knee. The vest is made of the same material as the jacket and the knickers. It has a row of silver buttons on each side of the opening. The shirt is made of white linen or cotton cloth, with whitework on the stand-up collar. A colored neck-scarf is tied in a bow and worn over the collar. Pattern-knitted stockings in black and white with garters in a variety of colors and black shoes are part of the costume. The bunad silver consists of a neck button or a neck pin for the shirt and all the silver buttons for the jacket, vest and knickers.

VESTFOLD

There is not much information available about the traditional folk costumes from Vestfold. Neither are there any folk costume pictures from Vestfold taken during the last century. Preserved antique costumes show that garments with modern design were in fashion in Vestfold. But Vestfold wanted a costume especially for use in connection with folk dancing in the early part of this century.

Klara Semb wrote in her book «For Country and City» in 1926, that many people from Østfold and Vestfold would like to know how to get information about antique costumes from their home districts. In respons to their questions, she showed them a picture of an antique costume from Vestfold, taken about 1890. She told them she was not quite sure, but the costume in the picture seemed to show details that resembled the antique Vestfold costume. Vestfold used to have more than one costume. The bunad that was designed in the 1930s was usually worn as a formal costume for the entire Vestfold district. The woman's bunad was re-designed 1945—56. At the same time, two additional bunads were designed for Vestfold. Different dance groups from Vestfold designed the man's bunad in 1937.

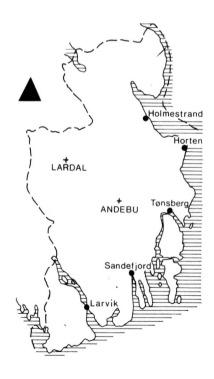

Picture of an old Vestfold costume believed taken in the 1890s. It is featured in Klara Semb's article «At the folk dance field» in the «For bygd og by» publication, 1926.

Woman's bunad from Vestfold

The idea of a formal costume for the entire Vestfold district surfaced about 1920—1930. Vestfold Husflidlag redesigned the bunad in 1954-1956 — that's when it got the design it has today. Since there is no known folk costume traditions in Vestfold, they had to choose from incomplete historical bunad materials. There are two different aprons for the bunad, both copied after antique aprons. One is copied after a striped-pattern, wool apron from 1895. The other is copied after a white cotton apron with a flower pattern from Haugberg in Andebu, from the first part of the 19th C. The whitework for the blouse was copied from antique shirt cuffs from Søby.

The skirt is made of black or blue wool material with a wide red border stripe, with a green-colored string around the edge, and a yellow string on the upper edge. Above the red border stripe there is a pattern-woven wool band. The skirt is pleated and the pleats meet in back. The bodice is made of green or red-colored frieze material and around the edges a pattern-woven wool band. It has a chain-laced bodice. The blouse is made of white linen with whitework around the collar and cuffs of the sleeves. It has two different aprons. We can choose from a striped pattern wool material or a white cotton apron with flower pattern embroidery in a variety of colors. The hat is made of black silk-brocade with red silk band and lace-work around the edge. It has silk bands that can be tied under the chin and a red bow in back. The belt is made of the same patterned wool band as we find in the bodice and the skirt. It has a silver buckle in front.

Red or white stockings and black shoes are part of the bunad. We use a short reversible cape of red and black wool material for the outdoors. The Vestfold bunad has its own silver design. Eyelets and a chain for the bodice, a ring-shaped neckpin and two brooches and button cufflinks for the blouse.

Man's bunad from Vestfold

In 1937 the Borre folk dance group took the initiative to design a man's bunad for Vestfold. The idea came from a jacket, now at the Norwegian Folk Museum, a pair of buckskin trousers from Andebu, owned by Vestfold District Museum, and a vest from Andebu. The bunad was redesigned in 1976. It is most popular in the northern and southern parts of Vestfold. It is made in two models — either with a black jacket and black knickers with red vest under, or red jacket and black knickers with a yellow colored vest under. The design is the same.

The jacket is made of black or red wool material. It has a row of metal buttons on each side of the jacket's opening and on the cuffs of the sleeves. A stand-up collar and turn-back lapels. The knickers are made of black wool material and with a flap in front. Either knickers or trousers can be used. The knickers have a waistband and a row of buttons by each knee. A vest made of yellow brocade material is used with the red jacket. For the black jacket, one uses the red vest.

The vest has a row of buttons on each side of the opening, with a stand-up collar and turn-back lapels. The shirt is made of white linen with whitework around the collar and cuffs of the sleeves.

A black hat or a red knitted cap is used. White patterned knitted stockings and black shoes are part of the costume. The bunad silver consists of neckpin and button cufflinks for the shirt, all the buttons for the bodice, the jacket and the knickers. The buttons can be made of either silver or pewter.

TELEMARK

The three areas Øst-Telemark, Vest-Telemark and Tinn all have different costumes. The costumes have changed a few times within each area, and the tailors often influenced the designs. A few folk costume models from Telemark are direct continuations of the antique costumes, from the second half of the last century. The Sash-skirt model from the eastern and western parts of Telemark, and the woman's bunad from Tinn, have always been in fashion as formal costumes, and they are the most recent models from these areas.

The man's bunad from Aust-Agder is copied from the «gråkufte-kleda» (grey-sweater costume). It has a short jacket with decorative trim and applique. It was in fashion from about 1850 until the last part of the 19th C, when the «short-fitted» jacket design became popular. The same costume is used as a man's bunad in Vest-Telemark. The formal costume for both Vest- and Øst-Telemark is designed from antique costumes, from the last part of the 18th C up until 1850. A red jacket was used with this costume, and it is therefore called «the red jacket costume». Anna Bamle began making bunads for Telemark in 1920, from antique costume design. «Den Norske Husflidsforening» in Oslo, and «Telemark Husflidsforening» later re-designed the bunad from antique costumes. The antique costumes used earlier had a larger variation in embroidery and other details, than the bunad model in use today. The Telemark bunads were favoured objects for artists like Johannes Flintoe, Adolph Tidemand and Erik Werenskiold in the last century. Antique costumes from different areas are preserved, and different museums around the country have many antique costumes from Telemark.

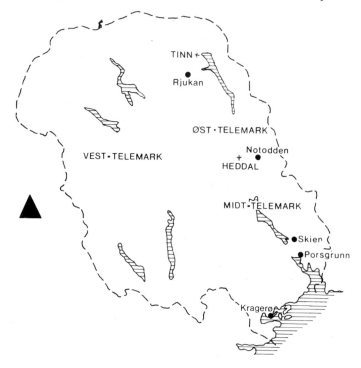

The congregation outside the Heddal stave church. Photo: Wilse (Norwegian Folk Museum).

Woman's bunad from Aust-Telemark

The Aust-Telemark costume was redesigned after the costume used in Aust-Telemark in 1820—1850. It got it's name «the red jacket» from the red embroidered jacket that was in use in the 18th C. Hulda Garborg was eager to have this bunad back in use. In 1920 Anna Bamle started to make bunads designed like the antique costumes known from her district, Heddal. They were called «the red jackets». Except for her rose embroideries on the skirts they had the same design as the bunads Telemark Husflidslag and Husflidsforeningen in Oslo designed. The bunad made by Husfliden has colored bands around the hem like the antique costumes used to have. Rose-embroidered friezesocks were a part of the old costume but they are seldom in use today.

The skirt is made of double shuttle weave wool material with red, blue and green borders around the hem. It is pleated and has a concealed pocket on one side. The bodice is made of red frieze material with rose embroidery on the front parts and in back. It has black rose pattern embroidered edges. The jacket is made of red double shuttle weave wool material with black rose embroidery in front and around the cuffs of the sleeves and a yellow edge around the hem. The jacket is short and wide. It is supposed to end above the belt to show off the belt. It closes with a hook. The blouse is made of white linen with embroidery around the collar and cuffs of the sleeves and in front. We can see from antique Telemark blouses that hardly any of them have the same embroidery. Both whitework and colored and black embroidery are used. The sash is about 3 inches wide, woven in a variety of colors. It is tied on one side in front. The apron is made of the same material as the skirt, with red edging and rose embroidery. Either the kerchief or woven bands, «bregda band», can be used. This model uses a kerchief with red embroidery. And around the kerchief is tied a silk scarf with the knot in front. The kerchief Anna Bamle designed was tucked and had narrow bands that could be tied in back. Also colored kerchiefs were used. Black stockings and black shoes with silver buckles are part of the costume. The bunad silver consists of silver eyelets for the bodice, a neck pin and two brooches and button cufflinks for the blouse. The Telemark silver used is filigree.

Woman's bunad from Telemark:
«Sash Skirt»

The «sash skirt» came into use about 1850, making it the most recent of the folk costumes from Telemark. As late as the 1950s older women still used the «sash skirt» for formal occasions. The young women of today who are using the «sash skirt» copied it from their grandmothers' bunads. There is a big difference in colors and embroideries in today's bunads. In the last part of the 19th C, the «sash skirts» used to be made of dark colored materials. The skirt and the apron had dark colored bands around the edges, and it got its name from the wide woven sash that goes around the waistline a few times.

The skirt is made of black wool material with a wide velvet hem. The border hem can be made in different colors. The bunad in the photos has one in red and black. The skirt is wide and finely pleated. The attached bodice is made of red velvet. It is open in front with silver eyelets on the back side of the opening. The jacket is made of dark colored wool material. It is very short and it is held together with a silver buckle. It has a stiffened edge in back. It is called «skjæl». The blouse is made of white linen with a high standing collar, and has embroidery in a variety of colors around the collar and in front. The cuffs of the sleeves can also be embroidered. One does not often see two blouses with the same embroidery. There are many antique blouses from Telemark that can be copied. The apron is made of the same material as the skirt. It has red velvet bands and a rose patterned embroidery around the border. Instead of the embroidery, one can use different patterned bands. The sash is made of woven wool yarn in a variety of colors. It is about 4 inches wide and about 80 inches long. It is wrapped a few times around the waist. They use a scarf tied with a knot in front or woven hair bands. Black stockings and black shoes are part of the costume. Also embroidered frieze socks are used. It is an old tradition. One also uses handmade shoes in various colors. The bunad silver consists of a neck pin and one or two brooches (called «slangesølje» or «bolesølje»). Button cufflinks for the blouse and eyelets for the bodice. The jacket has a silver buckle.

Man's bunad from Aust-Telemark

The «grey-colored» costume or the «short-fitted» jacket design are used in Aust-Telemark today. They were in regular use around 1840, but older men used them in this century also. A tailor by the name of O. A. Kolbjørnsrud (1834—1922) from Heddal designed the applique embroidery on the jacket. He also designed a green-colored jacket in addition to the regular white jacket. A few grey-colored costumes from Telemark are preserved. The decorations on the jackets vary.

The jacket is made of white frieze with edges, lapels and applique made of black wool material with red stitches. It is short with wedge-shaped insert in back and under the arms. It has a stand-up collar and turn-back lapels and a row of silver buttons on each side of the opening in front but it can not be buttoned. The pocket flaps and cuffs of the sleeves have silver buttons. Either knickers or trousers can be used. It is made of dark wool material and with a flap in front. The knickers have a waistband and cuffs with a row of silver buttons and a buckle on the outside of each knee. The vest is made of dark colored wool material. It has a row of silver buttons on each side of the opening, and also a few buttons higher up on the lapels so it can be buttoned all the way up. The shirt is made of white linen with whitework on the collar and cuffs of the sleeves and by the neck opening. The embroidery can be made in colors or whitework. A silk neck scarf can be used inside the shirt. White or black and white patterned knitted stockings and black shoes are part of the bunad. The bunad silver consists of a neck button or a neck brooch, button cufflinks and also a ring-shaped pin and all the silver buttons for the jacket, knickers and the vest. The buttons for this model are filigree.

Woman's bunad from Vest-Telemark

Like in Aust-Telemark, the formal costume for Vest-Telemark is a redesign of the folk costume from the first part of the 19th C. The «red jacket» came back in fashion. The folk costumes from Vest-Telemark changed in the 19th C. The last folk costume that was made had a skirt cut on the bias and a bodice with an attached insert. They were made in dark colors. When we compare the antique «red jacket» from old costumes and photos, with the new bunad, we can see that the old costume had a front insert. The old skirts did not have «rosesaum» — rose-embroidery. We can see from old pictures that they used a white kerchief with a colored scarf around the head, tied in a bow in front, or they used a colored kerchief. The antique costumes had a shorter bodice and jacket.

The skirt is made of black, double-shuttle weave wool material, with a red colored hem and a rose patterned embroidered border above the hem. The skirt is pleated. The bodice is made of green-colored cloth and red edges with rose patterned embroidery in front and back. The bodice is short and is chain-laced. The jacket is made of red wool material with rose-pattern embroidered bands around the cuffs and on each side in front. The jacket is open in front to show off the silver jewelry. The blouse is made of white linen with embroidery around the collar and cuffs of the sleeves and on each side of the neck-opening. It can be either whitework or colored embroidery. The apron is made of the same material as the skirt. It has red colored wool edges and a rose-pattern embroidery. The belt is a narrow, woven band; it goes around the waist twice and hangs down in front. The belt is supposed to be placed above the skirt's waistband. A black kerchief is used with the red jacket. A white kerchief is also used. It has whitework or colored embroidery and lace made in the «telebinding» technique. The kerchief has a roll of padding underneath. Some use antique colored silk scarves instead of the white kerchiefs. Woven bands for the hair are also used. The bunad silver consists of a neck pin, button cufflinks and one or two brooches, a «slange-brooch» or a brooch with dangles or a «bol-brooch». Eyelets and chain for the bodice. The Telemark-silver is usually filigree.

Man's bunad from Vest-Telemark

The «short tight-fitted» or the «rundtrøye-kleda» is used in Vest-Telemark. It is the most recently designed folk costume. Before the «short tight-fitted» design that came into fashion in the last part of the 1800s, they used the «grey-colored» jacket. It was different from the «grey-colored» jacket they used in Aust-Telemark. It did not have applique.

The jacket is called «rundtrøye» (short, tight-fitted). It is made of black wool material with turn-down collar and turn-back lapels. It has a row of silver buttons on each side in front and on cuffs of the sleeves, but it cannot be buttoned. Both knickers and trousers made of the same material as the jacket can be used. It has a flap in front. The knickers have a waistband, a buckle and a row of buttons on the outside of the knees. The vest has a row of silver buttons on eash side of the opening. It also has buttons on the lapels that can be buttoned. It is made of a black wool material. The shirt is made of white linen with whitework around the collar and cuffs of the sleeves. A colored silk neck scarf can be worn around the collar. It has knitted stockings in blue and white pattern. Some use patterned garters. These are tied under the cuffs leaving only the tassels visible. Black shoes with buckles are part of the costume. The bunad silver consists of the buttons on the jacket, vest and knickers. The buttons are often filigree. It has a button neck pin or just a silver pin.

Woman's bunad from Tinn

The Tinn-bunad of today is a continuation of the folk costume from 1850—1860. Then the antique «skjælingstrøya», the jacket with the stiffened edge, was replaced by the «wrapped bodice». It was thought to have been brought to Tinn by marriage from Numedal. The «skjælingstrøya» had a loose insert and the name means it had a stiff edge.

The bodice has an attached piece in front that wraps over to the other side and buttons. The decorative rose-pattern bands in back is an older detail than the «wrapped bodice». The rose-pattern embroidered bands are also used as decorations for the skirt and the apron. The embroidery is free-hand.

The skirt is made of black cloth with a rose embroidered border with a green colored stripe around the hem. It is pleated and is held up by rose embroidered suspenders. They are placed outside the bodice. The bodice is made of green colored cloth with black velvet edges and a «wrapper» that can be buttoned on the right side. The suspenders are placed outside the bodice. The rose embroidered band creates a v-shape in back. The jacket is now being redesigned. The blouse is made of white linen or cotton with white-work around the collar and cuffs of the sleeves. The apron is made of black wool damask. It has a rose embroidered border and a green colored band around the hem with the same embroidery as the skirt. The apron has woven bands in different colors with tassels hanging down on one side in front. The hat is made of black silk. It is tucked and has ribbons that can be tied under the chin. A black head scarf is tied in front. The bow can be sewed on the scarf or on a wide band.

The hat has again become popular. Black stockings and black shoes are part of the costume. The bunad-silver consists of one or two brooches, a neck button and button cufflinks.

AUST- AND VEST-AGDER

The traditional folk costume in Setesdal has been in use up until today. In the 1930s young girls used the every-day bunad as a school uniform. About that time young men and boys had changed to «city style» fashion. The Setesdal bunad kept it's popularity as a festive costume. The woman's bunad from Setesdal is one of the best preserved costumes, it has been in use since the last part of the 17th C. But the man's costume has been through a few changes. The most common man's costume consists of a pair of trousers and a short vest, designed about 1840. A costume for older men from Setesdal was re-designed. The differences in the costumes from Valle and Bykle are less noticeable.

In the last part of the 19th C, the Aust-Agder costume went out of fashion. The man's costume that came back into use in the 1920s, had really never been out of use, but the woman's costume had. Antique costumes from Åmli parish were used as copies for the re-design of the woman's bunad. It is named the Åmli bunad, but it was also called the Aust-Agder bunad. In addition to the man's bunad, which is a continuation of the most recent folk costume from this area, is a re-designed man's bunad, copied from antique costumes. In Aust-Agder, as in so many other areas, «The Young People's Society» has stimulated the interest in the use of the traditional costume. They conducted a bunad registration in Aust-Agder in 1910. The results were collected and

published in a pamphlet called «Antique costumes from Vest-Agder», Mandal 1929. Both women's and men's bunads from this area are copied from antique costumes.

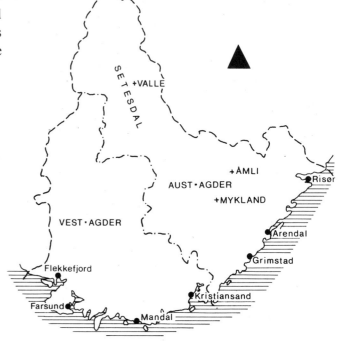

From Setesdal (After an old postcard. University library).

Woman's bunad from Valle in Setesdal

The woman's bunad from Setesdal is one of the bunads with the longest tradition. It is one of the oldest folk costumes in the country. The skirt has had almost the same design since the last part of the 17th C, and maybe even longer. The women from Setesdal wore a white frieze skirt with a leather belt around the waist for daily use. But they used a black skirt over the white one when they went to church or for other formal occasions. The brides used more than one skirt at a time. The costume they use today is the so-called «church costume». The embroideries vary. They are called «løyesømmen».

The bunad has two skirts — a white skirt under and a black skirt over. The black skirt has a straight front panel and is pleated in back. It has a stiffened bordered hem, two red and one green cloth bands around the hem. The skirt is finely pleated in back and gathered into a narrow breast-band in green with embroidery and red-colored edges in front. The skirt underneath is made of white wool material. It is not pleated in back. It is gathered into a narrow breastband and held up by short straps made of black cloth with embroidery and green edges in front. The stiffened hem is called «skoren». It has three different bands made of black cloth. The black skirt (the outer skirt) is so short that the stiff black hem (of the under-skirt) shows. The bodice is extra short. The black skirt has a black bodice with embroidery. Silver bands and a piece of red cloth in back. The white skirt has a white bodice with edges and straps made of black cloth decorated with wool yarn embroidery. The jacket is very short with wide sleeves. It is made of black cloth with green edges. It has embroidery in front, on the shoulders and on the cuffs of the sleeves. It has decorative silver bands on the cuffs of the sleeves and in back. There is a row of silver buttons on each side of the sleeves and a silver chain lacing the jacket together across the breast. The blouse is made of white cotton cloth with turn-down collar. It has tatting around the collar and cuffs of the sleeves. It can also be crochet-lace or lacework. They use a black kerchief with fringe. It can be solid black and it can also have embroidered or printed rose patterns. It is tied in a knot in front. They also use woven bands as head decorations. The bands hang down from underneath the kerchief. It has a woven belt or sash in red, yellow and green-colored wool yarn and a silver buckle «coat buckle». Black pattern knitted stockings, held up by leather straps with silver ornaments («sprette and sprota»). Black shoes are part of the bunad. A black shawl is used for the outdoors. It can be woven in two different patterns called «tæpe» and «tjeld». The bunad silver consists of neck buttons and button cufflinks and two or three brooches for the blouse. The largest brooch is placed highest up on the blouse. The breastband has silver buckles and the belt (sash) has a silver buckle. The jacket has silver buttons in front and on the cuffs of the sleeves. It closes with a jacket chain. The garters have silver ornaments called «sprette» and «sprota».

Man's bunad from Valle in Setesdal

The older men from Setesdal have used this traditional costume up until today, both for formal and daily use. This costume is a direct continuation of the folk costume tradition from the valley. Of the four different costumes from Setesdal, this particular bunad is the most recent one, in the period after the Reformation. It was in use about 1840, and, according to Johannes Skar, the tailor Nils Herbjørnsson from Tinn brought this man's bunad to the valley.

The buckskin patch in back is a more recent idea. Many people wondered why they used the buckskin patch. They thought it was copied after a foreign cavalry uniform, but there is no evidence of that.

The young men used a costume made of black cloth with green edges. The older men used a grey-brown costume with dark blue edges. Both young and old men used a black vest and a short grey jacket made of frieze. Around the turn of the century the men from Valle began to use a pattern-knitted sweater instead of the grey colored jacket in frieze.

The men from Setesdal could use short sleeves in summer. The black, high hat was replaced by a soft, black, felt-hat, about 1870. Old hat-forms, still exist, and one of them was used to make the hat in the photo (opposite page). The embroidery is by free-hand.

The black cloth trousers have been called «the world's longest trousers». They have long legs and reach high up in back, with a flap in front. They are held up by leather suspenders and cast brass buttons. The bib is made of green colored cloth with embroidery in a variety of colors and two rows of silver buttons. It has a buckskin patch in back called «skinnfoi», it continues in a thin leather stripe up the front. The sweater is knitted in a black and white pattern called «Setesdal pattern». It has black cuffs with green edges, embroidery and a row of silver buttons on each cuff. They wear the sweater inside the trousers and underneath the vest.

The vest is made of black cloth, with colored embroidery, a large silver buckle and a row of silver buttons on each side. The stand-up collar is embroidered, the back is made of white material. It closes with a silver filigree buckle. The shirt is made of white cotton cloth, with a turn-down collar edged with tatting. The hat is made of soft, black felt with a silver buckle and a silver chain around the crown. White patterned knitted stockings and black shoes with silver buckles are part of the bunad. The bunad silver consists of a neck button and a «horn ring» pin, a large silver, filigree buckle and two rows of silver buttons on the vest, the silver buttons on the bib, the cuffs of the trousers and on the cuffs of the sleeves of the sweater, a long watch chain around the neck, a silver chain around the hat and a silver buckle.

Woman's bunad from Åmli

The woman's bunad from Åmli came back in use about 1925—1926. The bunad had then been out of use for many years. A costume painting done by Johannes Flintoe about 1830 and antique costumes were used as copy for the new bunad. The jacket was copied after an antique jacket from Hillestad in Tovdal, made about 1830. The bodice was copied after an antique bodice found in Gjøvdal. The apron in the photo (opposite page) is copied after an antique apron from Vatne, the kerchief is from Mykland in Mykland. The originals dated about the first part of the 19th C. Many kerchiefs and aprons from the district are preserved, but they all have different patterns. Some of these costumes were in use in the last part of the 18th C. Silk and wool patterned aprons were being worn.

The skirt is made of black wool material with red and green borders. A thin red band around the hem, then a green border and a thin yellow band between the red and green borders. The skirt is pleated in back and tucked in front. The jacket is made of black wool material with red and green borders around the cuffs of the sleeves. The jacket is shorter in front and it has two pleats in back. It has a turn-down collar with a red colored edge and closes in front with two silver buckles. It has a row of silver buttons on each side of the jacket in front with button-holes made of a red colored head, but they are not cut open. The bodice is made of a red or green damask with patterned bands around the edges and decorative silver bands in back. It has a chain-laced bodice. The blouse is made of white linen with whitework on part of the shoulders around the collar and cuffs of the sleeves. The apron is made of white linen with wool yarn embroidery in a variety of colors and a fringe around the hem. The belt is made of a pattern-woven band with a silver buckle and the ends of the belt hanging down in front. The kerchief is made of white linen with wool embroidery in a variety of colors and with a red or white fringe. The kerchief's corners are put through a loop under the corner of the kerchief and then it is tied in a bow in front. Black or red stockings and black shoes with silver buckles are part of the costume. The bunad silver consists of a neck button, button cufflinks and one or two brooches for the blouse. The smallest brooch is placed highest up on the blouse. The different brooches are called: Rose-brooch, bol-brooch, slange-brooch and hjertesprette. Chain and eyelets for the bodice, silver buttons and silver buckles for the jacket, and a silver belt buckle.

Man's bunad from Åmli

In connection with the growing youth movement in the 1920s, this bunad came back into fashion. It was never completely out of use, they used the knickers with a flap in front up until the 1920s. It was customary in the eastern part of Aust-Agder to use it as a formal costume in the last part of the 19th C. They used trousers and a short, tight fitted jacket. The vest was copied after a groom's vest from Askland in Mykland, about 1833. The copy of the pattern knitted stockings came from Fiskvatn. The shoe buckles are copied after shoe buckles from Mjølhus in Froland.

The jacket is made of black wool material. It is short, with turn-down lapels and a row of silver buttons on each side in front, and a row of silver buttons on the cuffs of the sleeves. The jacket has a straight mid-seam in back and an oblique seam on each side of the mid-seam. It has knickers made of the same material as the jacket. The knickers have a flap in front and cuffs at the knees, and fastens with a silver button. There is a row of silver buttons on the outside of the knees. The vest is made of patterned brocade material. It has a stand-up collar, turn-down lapels and a row of silver buttons on each side in front. The shirt is made of white linen with whitework on the shoulders, around the collar and cuffs of the sleeves. They use a black or patterned neck scarf. The shirt collar turns down over the scarf. It also has pattern-knitted stockings, in black and white wool yarn, and garters in a variety of colors. Black shoes with large silver buckles are part of the costume. The silver consists of neck button, a «horn brooch» and all the silver buttons for the jacket, the vest and the knickers. The buttons are engraved, copied after antique buttons.

Woman's bunad from Vest-Agder

This bunad was designed in the first part of the 20th C. It was copied after an antique woman's costume from the period 1830—1870. Many people from the area had old costumes and bunad silver, and they also had a great deal of information about the costume. All the information about the bunad was collected and published in a booklet in 1929. The antique bodice could be made in different colors and materials. The embroideries on the shawl and purse could also vary.

The skirt is made of black wool material. It can be either pleated or tucked. It is held up by pattern-woven suspenders. The waistband is a narrow woven band, and a jacket is made of black wool material. The upper sleeves are wide and tucked while the cuffs are narrow. The jacket has the same style as the bodice. It closes with two silver buckles in front and it has a silver button on each cuff. The jacket is made of red, green or black wool damask. The jacket in the photos is made of damask material. It has a chain-laced bodice. The back of the bodice is gored to a flare.

The blouse is made of white linen with whitework in part of the shoulders around the collar and cuffs of the sleeves. The turn-down collar has tatting around the edge. It has a black wood apron with wool yarn embroidery in a variety of colors. The kerchief is made of white linen with drawnwork around the edges. Padding is used underneath the kerchief. The one used by women is called «vase» and the one for girls is called «rult». The kerchief is tied in back and the corners are supposed to hang down on the shoulders. It has a shawl made of black wool material with wool yarn embroidery in a variety of colors, and also a purse in black wool material with colorful wool yarn embroidery. Black or red stockings and black shoes with buckles are part of the costume. The bunad silver consists of a neck button, button cufflinks and one or two brooches for the blouse. One of them should be a large heart or ring-shaped brooch with large dangles. Eyelets and chain for the bodice; the chain is attached on one side with a pin. The jacket has silver buttons on the cuffs of the sleeves and silver buckles in front. The skirts' suspenders are fastened with silver buttons. The silver jewelry for this bunad were all copied after antique bunad silver from Vest-Agder.

ROGALAND

We do not know much about the folk costumes in Rogaland. But what we do know is that there was a difference in the clothing customs between Jæren and Inner Ryfylke during the last century, which indicates that there has been locally characteristic costumes in several places of Rogaland, if not all over the district.

But the Rogaland bunad is not a continuation of such a folk costume tradition. The man's bunad, as well as the woman's bunad, were designed during the 1920s, patterned after models at the Stavanger Museum. One of the prime forces behind the bunad work was Magnus Våge, the Rogaland Ungdomslag secretary. In his publication about the Rogaland bunad of 1929, he states that if one again were to use a «national bunad» in Rogaland, one had to utilize the museums. In the countryside the folk costumes had been forgotten already during the second half of the last century. At the Stavanger Museum large exhibits of costumes were featured in 1927/28 and 1948.

The model for the man's bunad was found at the Stavanger Museum: Two complete men's bunads from the beginning of the 19th C. The man's costume used today is identical with the one introduced in the 1920s, and has become the festive bunad for the whole district of Rogaland.

The woman's bunad appeared in the 1920s. The corset at the museum became the model of the eye on the bunad bodice. Of the old caps it was the so-called «påla» which was chosen for the new bunad. The woman's bunad underwent a revision in the 1950s. A bunad committee presented its proposal in 1955. According to this proposal the woman's bunad was to appear in various versions.

Still, in Rogaland one finds only one festive bunad.

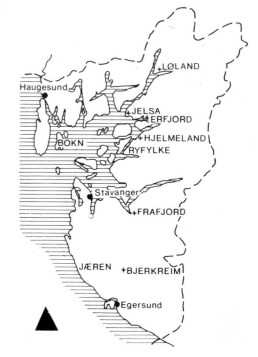

«A peasant wife from the Stavanger province» and «A peasant from the Stavanger province». J.F.L. Dreier: «Norwegian national costumes. 10 original drawings.» (University Library).

Woman's bunad from Rogaland

The Rogaland bunad was designed in the 1920s. A committee composed of representatives from Rogaland Bondekvinnelag, Haugesund and Omland Husflidslag, Stavanger Husflidsforening, Sauda Ungdomslag and Bondeungdomslaget from Stavanger got together and re-designed the bunad in 1955. Today's bunad can be made in many different colors, materials and have different embroideries. Antique costumes found at Stavanger Museum were copied to some extent out in the country. Complete costumes were not copied.

Very little is known about antique costumes from Rogaland. The district of Rogaland did not have any common costume in the old days. Many antique rose-embroidered (rosesaum), shawls and hats are known from different parts of the district. They have named the embroideries after the places where they were made, like: Løland, Bokn, Jelsa, Frafjord, Ersfjord, Bjerkreim and Tjelmeland, but they are also used outside these places. The original costume had an embroidery only on the shawl and hat, but later they have transferred it also to the apron and the purse, but they are not quite sure if that was used on the antique costumes. The bunad in the photos of the model from Rogaland has a brocade bodice and the embroidery is a copy from an antique hat from Jelsa. The «Nordaker Bunader» designed it. The costume can be made of different materials and have different embroideries.

The skirt is made of black, blue or green wool damask. It is pleated and has a patterned silk brocade bodice with black velvet and silver band trim. It has a chain-laced bodice. The blouse is made of white linen with white-work around the collar and cuffs of the sleeves. The apron, hat, shawl and purse are all made of the same material as the skirt and with the same embroidery from Jelsa. The hat has a silk band trim with color to match the bodice and also lace around the edge with a silver band above. It has silk ribbons that can be tied under the chin. The shawl has a silk fringe and is held together with a button connected with a chain in front. It has a purse with a silver or a nickel silver closing. The belt is made of black velvet with a silver buckle in front. They use a short cape made of the same material as the skirt for the outdoors. It can have embroidery around the stand-up collar. Black or red stockings and black shoes are part of the costume. The bunad silver consists of a button brooch with dangles, a brooch and button cufflinks for the blouse, eyelets and chain for the bodice, a silver belt buckle and a shawl button, and the silver or nickel-silver purse closing. The Rogaland bunad can use more than one type of bunad jewelry.

127

Woman's bunad from Rogaland

This is the second version of the woman's bunad from Rogaland, the version Husfliden in Stavanger designed in the 1950s. The bunad's flower-pattern embroidery was copied from an antique shawl from Løland.

The skirt is made of black, double-shuttle weave, wool material. It is pleated. The bodice is made of green or red wool damask. It has a chain-laced bodice. The blouse is made of white linen, with whitework around the collar and cuffs of the sleeves. The apron, the hat, the shawl and the purse are all made of the same material as the skirt. And they have the same wool yarn embroidery that was copied from the shawl from Løland. The hat has a lace ruche and a silver band around the edge. The shawl has a fringe around the edge and a button on each side of the shawl that is connected with a chain. The purse closing is made of silver or nickel silver. The belt is made of black velvet and has a silver buckle in front. Black or red stockings and black shoes are part of the bunad. For the outdoors one uses a short, black cape of double-shuttle weave wool material. The bunad silver consists of button cufflinks, button brooch, and a bigger brooch for the blouse, eyelets and chain for the bodice, belt buckle and two shawl buttons. The purse closing can be made of silver or nickel silver. Several silver designs have been made for this costume.

129

Man's bunad from Rogaland

Rogaland has only one man's bunad. Magnus Våge, the secretary of Rogaland Youth Association, and a tailor by the name of L. A. Sømme designed the bunad in the 1920s. It was copied after old male costumes from Stavanger Museum, dating back to the first part of the 19th C. The oldest known costume from Rogaland had knickers, a jacket and an overcoat. The jacket was exchanged for the vest in the last century. And the overcoat was made shorter, with a stand-up collar and small lapels, later it got a turn-down collar and wider lapels. The men used to have colorful costumes around the first part of the 1800s, but in the last part of the century the costumes changed to dark colors, and from knickers to trousers. When the man's bunad from Rogaland was reintroduced, it had been out of use for a long time.

The jacket is made of wool or other cloth. It has a stand-up collar and turn-down lapels, made of the same material as the vest. It has red trimming, a row of buttons on each side in front, on the pocket flaps and on the cuffs of the sleeves. But it cannot be buttoned. Either silver or pewter buttons can be used. The knickers are made of the same material as the jacket. One can wear either knickers or trousers. The trousers are called «lokabrok». The knickers have a row of buttons and a buckle on the outside of each knee. It has red trimming.

The vest is made of patterned silk brocade or green cloth. It has a row of buttons on each side of the opening in front, with a turn-down lapel and a stand-up collar. The shirt is made of white linen with whitework around the collar and cuffs of the sleeves.

Green knitted or white patterned knitted stockings and black shoes with buckles are part of the costume. The bunad jewelry consists of all the buttons for the jacket, vest and trousers, a button brooch and button cufflinks for the shirt, and silver shoe buckles. The bunad's jewelry was copied after an antique brooch and buttons from Rogaland. The buttons can also be made of pewter.

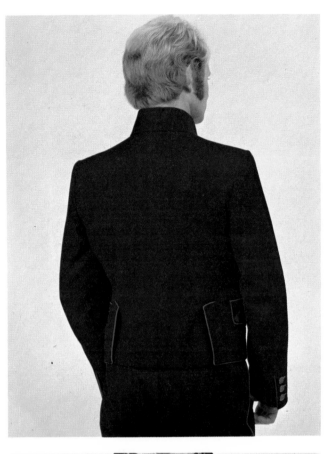

HORDALAND

Hordaland is undoubtedly the district of Norway where most bunads are found. Most of them are either a direct continuation of the folk costume tradition, or reconstructions based on preserved folk costume material. The festive costumes in Hardanger, Voss and Fana have never become outmoded. At Sotra, for instance, the older women were dressed in their traditional folk costumes down to the last war. In folk costume pictures from the last century, bunads from Hordaland are more often depicted than bunads from other parts of the country, and throughout the valleys a variety of folk costume material has been preserved.

Often, however, it is difficult to provide an overview of the bunads in this district. Not all costume areas are clearly defined, and inside one specific area one often finds several variations of one bunad. Thus, the Hardanger bunad is not identical in the outer and inner areas. In Nord-Hordland we find minor differences between the various rural townships. The women's costumes and the men's costumes have developed differently since the olden days. The man's costume has also not been as long in use as the woman's costume.

At the turn of the century, the «Hardanger National» became fashionable as the festive costume for women, even in districts where they had their own, traditional festive costumes. In several Hordaland areas the older generation of women went to church in their traditional festive garments, while the young ones dressed up in the «Hardanger National».

As the Hordaland bunads are partly a continuation of the folk costume tradition, and partly based on established folk costume material, the bunads have retained many details of the folk costumes. In the old days, one distinguished between costumes for married and unmarried women, and today several of the bunads maintain this difference. In the inner areas the married women wore a head shawl, while in the outer areas various kinds of the so-called «blue cap» have been common, but also here the women have had their special «church shawls». Earlier, the jacket belonged to the festive costume, but several Hordaland bunads still feature a jacket for the women.

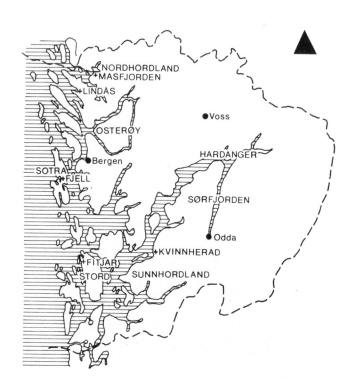

«Coastal peasants at Bergen». Joachim Frich: «Norwegian National Costumes». Christiania 1847.

Woman's bunad from Stord and Fitjar

When the home-craft school at Stord started in 1947, the first project was to make their own bunad. Gunvor Trætteberg and teacher Øydis Eide Høyland were in charge. The copy of the woman's bunad, from the last century, used to have a blue hat, («blåhuve») a jacket with a peplum, and underneath a chain-laced bodice. Older women used it in this century also, and the costumes were made of preserved materials.

The skirt is made of double-shuttle weave, wool material. It is hand-pleated. The jacket has a peplum made of the same material as the skirt, it has vegetable-dyed, woven wool bands. It closes in front with concealed hooks. The bodice is made of red, double-shuttle weave, wool material, with vegetable-dyed, woven wool bands. It has a chain-laced bodice, with an insert inside the bodice. The insert can either be woven or embroidered, with a blue edge made of the same material as the skirt, or silk. The blouse is made of white linen with whitework around the collar and cuffs of the sleeves. The apron is made of a woven material mix of cotton, linen and wool, with patterns called «krokbragd» and «smettborder». The hat is a copy of the antique «blue-caps». It is made of blue wool material with white lace around the front edge, and a woven band around the crown. This model has a belt with gold-filled ornaments with dangles. An embroidered belt with a buckle can also be used.

Black or blue stockings and black shoes are part of the costume. The bunad silver consists of a neck button and one or two gold-filled brooches. A necklace («dalakjede») may also be worn. The belt has gilded ornaments, the eyelets and chain are made of silver.

Woman's bunad from Sørfjorden in Hardanger

The Hardanger bunad is the most famous of all the Norwegian folk costumes. In the national romantic era, around the last part of the 19th C, it became a national costume, and it was copied all over the country, but usually simplified. But Hardanger has kept the old costume traditions, the formal costume for women was never out of use. The costume and their use differ from district to district in Hardanger. This is a formal woman bunad from Sørfjorden. Within the same district they have different ways of putting the costume together. The embroidery on the blouse and apron may be different, and also the insert, belt and the bands that hang down from the belt in front. They may be woven or beaded in different patterns and techniques. Straw-beads and small, round beads are used. There is a difference between the woman's bunad and the young girl's bunad. The women use a headdress and a silver belt, and look more dressed up for formal occasions than the young girls. Hardanger women also have a winter bunad.

The skirt is made of black or dark wool material. It may have a red or green hem, and is pleated. Farthest out in Hardanger they use a tucked skirt. It has a red or green bodice made of either cloth or brocade material, with home woven, rose-patterned trim. The bodice is open in front with a loose insert. It can be closed with two or three hooks at the waistline in front. The insert may be made in different patterns and colors. The one in the photo is made of small straw beads on a red colored insert. The blouse is made of white linen or cotton cloth with whitework or black stitch embroidery around the collar, on each side of the placket and on the cuffs of the sleeves. The apron used for formal occasions is made of white linen or cotton cloth, with Hardanger embroidery. It has a belt with gilded ornaments and a buckle in front. The belt also has three, long streamers hanging down in front. The one in the middle is called «fanglenja» and the ones on each side are called «breida-band». The women's headdress is called «fedla», it is a white pleated kerchief, with a roll of padding made of plywood, lined with linen underneath. It is tied in back with two red bands. The kerchief is fastened with two, long white cotton bands, and a band of whitework is tied around the kerchief. Black stockings and shoes are part of the costume. They use a cape in a dark color with red lining, for the outdoors. The bunad silver consists of a neck button with dangles, button cufflinks and a brooch for the blouse. The belt has silver ornaments and a silver buckle. And on the streamer in the middle («fanglenja») there are decorative silver ornaments. An Agnus Dei pendant is supposed to hang in a silver chain that reaches the belt. The silver jewelry for the Hardanger bunad should be gilded, except for the neck button and button cufflinks. But the dangles on the neck button are usually gilded.

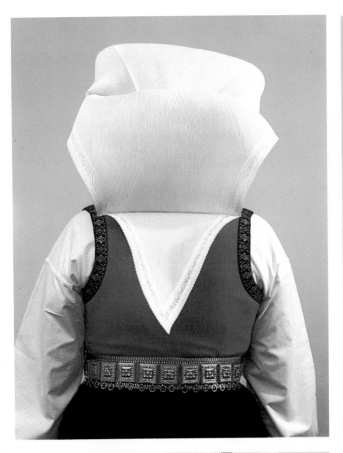

Young girl's bunad from Ullensvang in Hardanger

For over a hundred years it has been a tradition that the girls of Hardanger wear a bunad when they are confirmed. The differences between the woman's and the girl's bunad are these: women wear a kerchief, the girls use hair bands; the silver belt with the streamers hanging down in front, and also the Agnus Dei pendant are reserved for married women. The girls are not supposed to dress up like the married women.

The skirt is made of black or dark blue wool material. In the inner part of Hardanger, they use pleated skirts, while farthest out in Hardanger, the skirts are tucked. It has a red or green bodice made of wool or brocade material, with home-woven rose-patterned trimming. The bodice is open in front, with a loose insert. The insert can be embroidered in different patterns and colors. This particular insert is embroidered with beads. The blouse is made of white linen or cotton cloth, with whitework or black stitch embroidery around the collar, on each side of the placket and on the cuffs of the sleeves. It has a white linen or cotton apron with a wide Hardanger embroidery. The belt is embroidered. «Fangbånd» streamers hanging down in front can be used. In the old days, they were made narrower than the ones worn by adult women.

The girls use a rose-patterned hair ribbon with red tie bands in wool that have a beaded pattern at the ends. Black stockings and black shoes are part of the costume. A dark colored cape made of wool material, with red lining is used for the outdoors. The bunad silver consists of a neck button with dangles, button cufflinks, a brooch for the blouse, and a silver buckle for the belt. Except for the neck button and the button cufflinks, the rest of the jewelry is gilded.

Woman's winter bunad from Ullensvang

In winter time in Hardanger, they use a jacket called «sneatrøya». It has an apron with inserted black stitch embroidery. They do not use the silver belt with this bunad. The winter bunad varies a little from district to district in Hardanger. This bunad is from Sørfjorden.

The pleated skirt is made of black wool material. The jacket is made of black wool material, and has home woven edges, made in a rose pattern. It is open in front with a loose insert. The insert can be embroidered in different patterns and colors. One can also use a beaded pattern. This insert's embroidery is called «smøyg». A neck bib is used inside the jacket instead of a blouse. It has black stitch embroidery around the collar and on each side of the neck opening.

The apron is made of a fine, black material with inserted black stitch embroidery. The belt is embroidered and has a silver buckle. The belt in the photos (opposite page) has the same embroidery as the insert. The embroidery can be made in different colors and techniques. This bunad does not have silver belt or bands hanging down from the belt (fangbånd). It has a white kerchief for women. Black stockings and black shoes are part of the costume. The bunad silver consists of a neck pin with dangles, a gilded silver brooch, and a gilded silver buckle for the belt.

Woman's bunad from Kvinnherad

Since the women who are using the Kvinnherad bunad today can remember relatives who never wore any other costume than the bunad, they can be very sure of style and tradition. And the artists, J. Frich, G. Prahl, and J. F. Eckersberg painted the woman's bunad from Kvinnherad about 1800. So we can compare the costumes of today with the ones in the paintings. Married and unmarried women use different head-dresses. Both women and girls wore the blue hat daily, but for formal occasions the women wore a kerchief while the girls used a white hat. The photos show both the white hat for girls and the kerchief for women. The blue hat shown on page 145 is to be worn with the winter bunad. In the last century, two different jackets were used. A wool jacket for daily use. But for formal occasions, they wore the «laskatrøye», with the same type of jacket as is used today, over the red bodice. Both the insert and the trim can be made in many different patterns and colors, either embroidered or woven.

The skirt is made of black wool material, with a tucked part in back, about 3 inches down from the waistline. It has a bodice made of red wool material, with woven or embroidered trimming. The bodice is open in front, with two hooks at the waistline. It has a loose insert in front. The jacket is made of black wool material, it has a peplum with a gore at both sides and in the middle of the back. It is low cut in front and can be closed with hooks. It has a white linen or cotton blouse with whitework around the collar and cuffs of the sleeves. The apron is made of white linen with Hardanger embroidery. Either an embroidered or woven insert may be worn; the one in the photo is embroidered. It has geometric patterned embroidery, in a variety of colors. The headdress is a white kerchief made of linen, with a roll of padding underneath and under that, a loose, white piece of cloth. The headdress has a white embroidered band, tied in back. The girls use the «white hat», which has a roll of padding underneath, and is fitted to the head, with bands tied in back. And a white embroidered band is tied in a bow in back.

A patterned scarf can also be used with this bunad. It is folded so the corners cross in back and also in front, and the corners are put inside the jacket in front. Red stockings with an eight-leaf, rose pattern and black shoes are part of the costume. A plaid shawl with fringe is used for the outdoors. The bunad silver consists of a neck button and colored stone brooch. In the old days, they used smaller brooches. The bunad silver should be gilded.

Winter bunad from Kvinnherad

The wool jacket came back in fashion for Kvinnherad's winter bunad. It used to be worn in the last century, along with a finer formal jacket called «laskatrøya». The «blue hat» goes with the winter bunad, like it used to in the 19th C. It is worn by both married and unmarried women.

The skirt is made of black wool material, and is finely pleated in front. The jacket is copied after the antique wool jacket. It is made of black wool material with red patterned woven bands. The jacket is waist-length, with wide tucked sleeves and is open in front. It also has a loose insert. The blouse is made of white linen or cotton and it has whitework around the collar, on each side of the placket and on the cuffs of the sleeves. An ascot may also be used.

The insert is made of black wool material with red patterned woven trimming. It has a black wool or cotton apron with different colored thin striped pattern. It also has a woven belt made in the same pattern as the insert's trim. The hat is made of blue wool material. It has a roll or padding with a white piece of linen underneath. When the hat is on, a little white front edge is supposed to be visible. It also has a woven band tied in back. A plaid shawl is used for the outdoors. The bunad silver consists of a neck button and one or two brooches of oxidized silver.

Woman's bunad from Fana

The formal costume from Fana has never been out of use. Antique costumes and pictures are preserved, so we know how the costumes used to look. The antique costume could have either an embroidered, beaded or woven insert in different colors and patterns. Different patterns and techniques were used on the antique white aprons. There always used to be a difference between the woman's bunad and the girl's bunad, and they still try to keep this difference. When they get married, they change the blue hem on the skirt with a green hem, and they can use a silver belt and the bunad jewelry can have stones in red, green and violet colors. They will also have to use a kerchief, which is made higher than the one used in the last century.

The skirt is made of black or dark blue wool material with a green hem. It is finely pleated. The jacket is made of black or dark blue wool material with flower patterned trim. It is open to the waistline. The bodice is made of red damask or wool material with velvet or silk trimming. Some use green colored trim, like they used in the mid 19th C or a blue trim like that of a young girl's bunad. It is open with a loose insert in front. The insert can be made in different patterns and colors. The bunad in the photo has a wool yarn embroidered insert with a green velvet trim. It has a white linen or cotton cloth blouse, with whitework in different techniques, or in cotton cloth with crochet, lace or embroidered insert. It can have a woven or embroidered belt, in different patterns and colors, with or without streamers with fringe. The married women also can use a silver belt. They wear a kerchief, made of white cotton cloth, which has a roll of padding underneath. The long tie bands have embroidery, crochet or tatting at the ends. Black pattern knitted stockings and black shoes with buckles are part of the costume. The bunad silver consists of a neck button and button cufflinks, one or two brooches and a silver buckle for the belt. Married women can also use a belt with silver ornaments and a silver pendant. The bunad silver is usually gilded. Married women can also use different colored stones in their jewelry. It is an old saying that only married women could use green colored stones.

146

Young girl's bunad from Fana

For a time it was believed that the young girl's bunad was the original Fana bunad. However, there is a difference between the women's and girls' bunads. The headdress, trimming and bunad jewelry are not the same. While the women wear a kerchief, girls can use a hair band, called «rogge-bånd». The trimming on the bodice and skirt, and often also the insert on the girls' bunad should be made in a blue color. The women use a green trimming. The silver belt and pendant are used only by adult women. It is an old saying that young girls should not use green colored stones on their belts. Otherwise, the women's bunad and the girls' bunad are alike.

The skirt is made of black or dark blue material, with a blue colored silk or velvet hem. It is finely pleated. The bodice is made of red wool, damask or velvet with blue silk trim. Inside the blue silk trim there is a decorative beaded band. The bodice is open with an insert in front. Either wool yarn embroidery or a beaded insert can be used. It often has a blue trim. The blouse is made of white linen or cotton cloth, with whitework around the collar, on each side of the placket and on cuffs of the sleeves. It has an apron made of white linen, with whitework in different techniques, or a cotton apron with inserted crochet, lace or embroidery. On the apron shown in the photo, «Hedebo-seam» has been used.

The belt can be either woven or embroidered. This particular bunad-belt is embroidered with beads and wool yarn on canvas. Hair ribbons are worn. Since so few girls have long hair these days, they have made artificial hair, out of material, and braided hair ribbons around it. It is put up on the head in a loop. Black stockings and black shoes with buckles are part of the costume. The bunad silver consists of a neck button, with a red stone and button cufflinks, a brooch, and a silver buckle for the belt. It should be gilded. The girls are not supposed to have as many stones in their jewelry as the women.

Man's bunad from Fana

This male bunad is a copy of the costume which was in use about 1830—1850. Around the turn of the century, the folk costume for men was almost out of fashion. Some old men continued to use knickers and the antique fashioned jacket. And some young men wore the tight-fitted vest and trousers like the more recent folk costume. About 1900—1920, the male bunad with knickers and two vests came back in fashion, in connection with activities in the farm youth organization.

It is a medium-length jacket, made of white or dark frieze with gores in the back. The jacket does not have any collar. It is held together with a «blind-hook» connected with a silver or pewter chain. Knickers made of black wool material, with a buckle and a row of buttons on the outside of each knee are part of the male bunad. The button holes are made of red and yellow wool yarn. The knickers have a flap in front. Two vests are used at the same time. The first vest is made of red wool material with green trimming and green and yellow button holes. It has no collar, but has two rows of silver buttons in front. The second vest should be made of black or dark blue material with red trimming and red and yellow button holes. This vest has a high standing collar with red applique embroidery. It has two rows of buttons, but this vest should not be buttoned. Both vests have eight-leaf rose patterned embroidery, or other embroidered patterns on the pocket flaps. The shirt is made of linen or cotton with whitework around the collar and cuffs of the sleeves. With the costume goes a high hat, made of stiffened black wool felt. White pattern-knitted stockings and black shoes with buckles are part of the costume. The bunad silver consists of a neck button, and button cufflinks and also a pin placed under the neck button, and all the silver buttons for the vest, the knickers and the buckles by the knee cuffs.

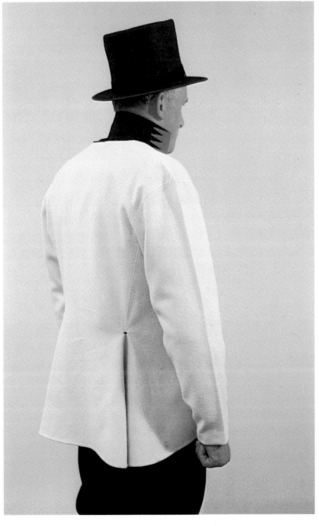

Woman's bunad from Sotra

Up until the Second World War, some women still used the traditional costume in Sotra. It had a blue hat, dark colored skirt and overcoat, and a red bodice with a green jacket underneath. A special shoulder scarf was used for church, called a «white cloth», folded corner to corner.

Right after the Second World War, the Sotra homemakers committee redesigned the bunad. They had a secure foundation to build upon, because many people still had antique costumes in their possessions. These antique costumes were displayed in Bergen. They chose the formal costume, a green bodice with a red jacket under. Some used a white kerchief. Traditionally, the women from Sotra only used the kerchief for church. Both women and girls used the «blue hat».

The skirt is made of black wool material, and has a green hem with a yellow thin band above. It is finely pleated, with a fastened pleated piece right underneath the waistband. The jacket is made of red cloth, with flower patterned silk bands or yellow or green bands around the cuffs of the sleeves and around the opening in front. The bodice is made of green cloth, with bands and beaded bands around the edges. It has an open, chain-laced bodice, worn outside the jacket. With a «bora buckle» on each side of the opening and a loose insert in front. The insert has a beaded pattern, with a black velvet trim. The blouse is made of white linen with whitework around the collar, on each side of the placket, and on the cuffs of the sleeves. It has an apron made of «gloria yarn». Wool aprons are customary. Right now a head dress is being created for the bunad, and it will be a copy of the antique white kerchief worn to church. The blue hat will not be redesigned, instead, they will use a roll of padding underneath. It has a belt made of red cloth, with gilded ornaments. Black stockings and black shoes are part of the costume. The bunad silver consists of a neck button, and a brooch, silver eyelets and a chain, and two, gilded «bora buckles». The belt has gilded ornaments and a buckle. An Agnus Dei silver pendant is worn with this bunad.

Woman's bunad from Voss

The formal costume from Voss was never out of use. The bunad used today is a continuation of the formal costume, from about the middle of the last century. But it has changed some, of course. About 1870—1880, the women from Voss started to use the kerchief from Hardanger, instead of the kerchief, «nastduken», from Voss. There is a difference between the women's and the young girls' formal costume. The married women wear a kerchief, «nastduk», and they have a black stitch embroidery on the blouse, and also a green colored hem with a silver band above. The young girls have velvet bands on their skirts. The silver belt and neck chain can be used only by married women.

The skirt is made of dark blue, double shuttle weave wool material, with a green hem and silver lace above. The skirt is pleated. The bodice is made of red cloth with green trimming, and a beaded band. It has an open bodice with a loose insert in front. The insert has a beaded pattern with a black velvet trim. Voss women use only square patterns in the insert. The blouse is made of white linen or cotton cloth, with black stitch embroidery around the collar, on each side of the placket and on the cuffs of the sleeves. It has an apron made of white linen or cotton, with a wide embroidered border called, «utskurdsaum». The headdress for women is a stiffened kerchief, «nastduken». For formal occasions a stiffened kerchief with black stitch embroidery, called «svartnastduk», is used. The two different embroideries used today are called «rose pattern» and «neck hook». The embroidery on the kerchief shown in the photo is called «neck hook» embroidery. The kerchief (nastduken) has a roll of padding tied over a piece of plywood covered with leather. The belt for women has silver ornaments and a silver buckle in front. Black stockings and black shoes are part of the costume. A cape or a plaid wool shawl can be used for the outdoors. The bunad silver consists of a neck button with dangles, a «bowl brooch» and a belt with silver ornaments and a silver buckle. The silver bowl brooch and the silver belt are usually gilded and with red stones. They also wear coin-type pendant, which is fastened with a hook on the insert.

Young girl's bunad from Voss

When the young girls from Voss are confirmed, they keep up the old tradition and wear a bunad. The young girl's bunad is different from the women's bunad in many ways, which has always been the case. The women wear a kerchief, «nastduk», but the young girls do not use anything on their heads. They wore hair bands, called «svorteborda», with their formal costumes in the last century. Braids put up in loops with bands around and kerchiefs are also used. And also a head-dress called «kueplagget» used to show the shame of an unmarried mother. The girls' skirt has three velvet bands, and was in use in the 1870s and 1880s. When they get married, the girls change the velvet bands to a green trim with silver lace. The girls' blouses have whitework and their belts have a beaded pattern. Only the married women can have a silver belt and a neck chain.

The skirt is made of a dark blue, double shuttle weave wool material with three velvet bands a little above the hem. It is pleated. The bodice is made of red cloth, with green trimming and beaded bands. The bodice is open in front with a loose insert. It has a beaded pattern with a black velvet trim.

The blouse is made of white linen or cotton material with whitework around the collar, on each side of the placket and on the cuffs of the sleeves. It has an apron made of white linen or cotton material with wide embroidery above the hem, called «utskurdsaum». The young girls wear nothing on the head. The bunad has a pattern-beaded belt with a silver buckle in front. Black stockings and black shoes with buckles are part of the bunad. The bunad silver consists of a neckbutton with dangles, a brooch and a silver belt buckle.

Winter bunad from Voss

All the traditional costumes have a jacket. They used two different jackets at Voss around the latter part of the 19th C, they were called «rukketrøya» and «breidtrøya». Around 1880 only the jacket called «breidtrøya» was used, and it is still worn as a jacket for the bridal costume. Either jacket can be used with the winter bunad. The married women wear a white kerchief, called a «white cloth».

The skirt for women is made of dark blue, double shuttle weave wool material, with a green colored hem called «kvare». It is pleated. The young girls use the formal skirt (festdossa) as part of the winter costume. The jacket is made of black wool material. One type has tucked sleeves with a single row of buttons in front, called «rukke-trøye», or it can have a «breidtrøye», a jacket with an embroidered insert. Under the jacket there is an ascot. It has whitework around the collar, on the cuffs of the sleeves and on each side of the placket.

The apron is made of black wool material with embroidery and also embroidered bands that can be tied in back. Married women wear stiffened white kerchiefs with embroidery, called «utskurdsaum». Underneath the kerchief, there is a roll of padding made of plywood covered with leather. Black stockings and black shoes with buckles are part of the costume. The bunad silver consists of a neck button and a bowl-brooch for the blouse, silver buttons and a thick neck chain.

Man's bunad from Voss

This bunad came back in fashion about the 1920s. The short, fitted jacket, «rundtrøya», was in regular use in Voss in the middle of the 19th C. Around 1860 trousers came into use, instead of knickers. Around the turn of the century, the men stopped wearing the antique costume. Voss has both a man's bunad and a boy's bunad. The boy's bunad has a vest with a single row of buttons in front and a pair of knickers, while the man's bunad has a vest with a row of buttons on each side of the opening in front, and either knickers or trousers.

The jacket is made of cloth or frieze. It has a stand-up collar, turn-down lapels and a row of silver buttons on each side of the front opening, and on the cuffs of the sleeves. The jacket cannot be buttoned. Either knickers or trousers can be worn. They are made of the same material as the jacket and have a flap in front, a buckle and a row or silver buttons on the outside of each knee.

The shirt is made of white linen or cotton material with whitework around the collar and cuffs of the sleeves, with a red vest made of cloth that has green colored trim around the collar. It is open in front with a row of silver buttons on each side. It has a green insert in front, with two rows of buttons with button holes. There are two vests. White patterned knitted stockings with garters in a variety of colors, and black shoes are part of the bunad. The bunad silver consists of a neck button with dangles and silver buttons for the jacket, the vest and the trousers. A watch chain in silver is often used.

Woman's bunad from Osterøy

Only the headdress and smaller details vary in the different parts of Nordhordaland. This is the woman's bunad from Osterøy. This design is copied from an antique costume dating back to the last part of the 19th C. It was the formal costume, primarily used for weddings. It has a red bodice, white sleeves and a white apron. For less formal occasions, they wore a blue colored bodice and a green jacket. The women's headdress was a white linen hat and the young girls wore head bands. The antique costumes used either woven, embroidered or beaded inserts.

The skirt is made of black or dark blue wool material with a green colored hem. It is finely pleated. The bodice is made of red cloth, with silk trim, rick-rack and beads around the edges. It is open in front with a loose insert, with a silverfilled «bora-buckle» with dangles on each side of the opening. Around the «bora-buckles» there is a beaded decoration.

The insert is made in a lacy beaded pattern with red cloth under and a green velvet trim. They also use embroidered inserts. The blouse is made of white linen with whitework around the collar, on each side of the placket and cuff of the sleeves. It has an apron made of white linen with whitework. The woman's bunad has a belt with silver ornaments. A white linen hat is used with it. It is placed on a roll of padding and is tucked in back with embroidery or a monogram around the tucked end. Black stockings and black shoes are part of the costume. The bunad silver consists of a neck button and a brooch, and «bora buckles» for the bodice, a belt with silver ornaments and a silver buckle. All the silver is gilded.

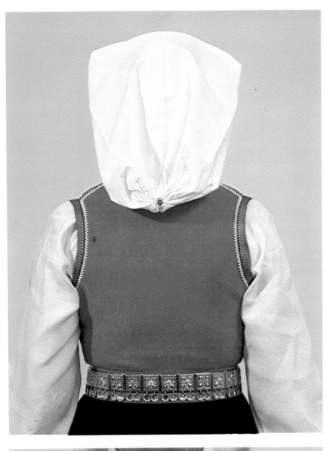

Man's bunad from Nordhordaland

The actor Johan Øvretveit brought the Nordhordaland bunad back into fashion in the 1920s. It is now used all over Nordhordaland, except for a few variations in the different districts. This bunad is copied after a male costume from the first part of the 1800s. The men stopped wearing the traditional costume in the late 19th C, but the women used it for decades.

The jacket is made of black wool material with green trimming and green button holes. The button holes are not opened. It has a row of metal buttons on each side of the opening in front, but it cannot be buttoned. The jacket has a seam down the center of the back. The knickers are made of the same material as the jacket. They have a flap in front with three buttons and there is a button on each pocket flap. The cuffs of the knickers have a buckle and a row of buttons on the outside of each knee.

Two vests are worn for this bunad. Inside is worn a green cloth vest with red trimming and red button holes. It has two rows of buttons and is always buttoned. Outside this, is used a red vest with a stand-up collar, green button holes and trimming. It too has double rows of buttons, but they are not buttoned. The red vest can also have a green insert, making it look like two vests, as in the photos on the opposite page. The shirt is made of white linen with whitework around the stand-up collar and cuffs of the sleeves. It has a red knitted hat, with a green napped trim. The garters are tied under the cuffs leaving only the tassels visible. The bunad silver consists of a neck button and button cufflinks. All the buttons on the jacket, the knickers and the vest can be made of either silver, brass, or pewter.

Woman's bunad from Masfjorden

The first Masfjord bunad was redesigned in the latter part of the 1940s. The apron was copied after a 150 year old pattern-woven apron. The antique church hat, made of black silk, became the hat model for the married women. In the old days, the women from Masfjorden used a white hat. The young girls used bands as hair decorations. A piece of the striped, woven apron material is used to make a belt for the girl's bunad. The bodice is copied after an antique bodice, but the pattern for the woven edges is copied from the striped apron.

The skirt is made of dark blue wool material, with woven border bands. It is pleated. The bodice is made of the same material as the skirt and has the same woven trimming. It has three decorative buckles on each side of the opening in front, called «bora buckles». The bodice has an insert in front, it is made of linen and has cross-stitch embroidery. The blouse is made of white linen whitework around the neck and on each side of the placket and on the cuffs of the sleeves.

It has a home-woven apron in a striped pattern half-woolen material. The hat for women is made of black silk with white lace around the front edge. Young girls use a woven hair band. Both are shown in the photos. The belt for married women is made of red cloth with silver ornaments and a silver buckle in front with a «bora buckle» on each side. Black stockings and black shoes with buckles are part of the costume. The bunad silver consists of a small neck brooch and a larger brooch, «bora buckles» on the bodice, and the silver buckle on the belt. This is for the women's bunad. The young girls wear a silver buckle on the woven belt. The silver belonging to this bunad is not gilded.

SOGN AND FJORDANE

In the district of Sogn and Fjordane, we distinguish between the bunads of Sogn, Sunnfjord and Nordfjord. But within each of these areas the costume customs have varied from township to township, and the costumes have changed over time.

In Sogn, the white woman's cap has been featured as a festive garment in an unbroken tradition up until today. Otherwise, the use of a traditional folk costume ended at the turn of the century. The woman's bunad, however, was again worn in several Sogn areas early in this century. The woman's bunad of today builds on the folk costumes as they were used in the inner and central parts of Sogn. In 1925 a special woman's bunad was composed for Brekke in the outer part of Sogn.

We have many variations of the woman's bunad from Sunnfjord. Most of the background material is found in Jølster where Olina Fossheim already in 1914 began the work on a special Jølster bunad. At that time, a generation which had worn the old costumes was still alive. One could, in other words, build on both the preserved costume material as well as oral tradition. The man's bunad in Sunnfjord was designed in 1960, patterned after models in the museums in Sunnfjord and Bergen.

The man's as well as the woman's bunads in Nordfjord appeared in the 1920s. The Firda Ungdomslag appointed in 1947 a bunad committee to research what could be found of old costume material and revise the bunads from the 1920s. Several artists copied the costumes in Sogn, Sunnfjord and Nordfjord from the last century, partly by building on each other's pictures. Much old costume material is preserved in the museums and throughout the districts.

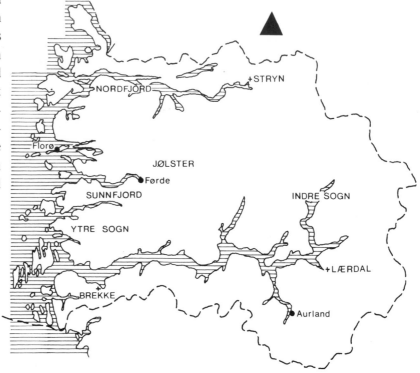

«Costumes from inner Sogn». Chr. Tønsberg: «Norwegian National Costumes». Christiania 1852.

Woman's bunad from Aurland in Sogn

The woman's bunad from Sogn is a continuation of the antique woman's costume from the last part of the 18th C, but also from the 19th C. It was copied after old preserved costumes and pictures. In the 1820s, Johannes Flintoe drew pictures of different Sogn costumes for both women and girls. Different skirts and bodices, with jackets or blouses under, distinguish the two. The young girls used either scarves or bands in their hair, and the women wore a white hat. The women's hat from Sogn has never been out of use. In Aurland, some women continued wearing the hat long after the folk costume was out of use. In the last part of the last century the folk costume was not worn any longer. But it came back into use in different areas in the first part of this century. The difference between the women's and the girls' costume is the women's headdress. Head bands and a different belt are used for the girls' bunad. A green silk blouse can also be worn with the women's costume.

The skirt is made of black wool material with a colored hem. It usually has a green hem, with embroidery or applique, but it can also be made in other colors. The skirt can be tucked or finely pleated. It has a bodice made of patterned brocade with black velvet trim. It is a chain-laced bodice. Two different blouses can be used with the Sogn bunad. The white linen blouse shown in the photos has both whitework and black stitch embroidery around the collar in front and on the cuffs of the sleeves. It can also be just whitework or just black stitch embroidery. The bunad also has a green blouse with white tucked sleeves and narrow cuffs. This blouse is worn only by married women. It has a black colored cotton apron with a striped pattern. Married women use a stiffened thin cotton hat, called «hodnhua». A wide stiffened band of tucked lacework is tied around the hat and above this, a patterned silk scarf, with a bow in the front. The young girls wear hair bands. Women use a belt with silver ornaments and a silver buckle. A black velvet belt with a silver buckle is used with the girls' bunad. The purse is made of black wool material and it has a silver closing. Black stockings and black shoes are part of the costume. The bunad silver consists of a neck pin with dangles, a large brooch, silver eyelets and chain for the bodice, a silver belt with a silver buckle and a purse closing of silver.

Man's bunad from Sogn

This bunad is copied after a man's costume from the last century. From the first part of the 19th C until 1860, it was customary for men from Sogn to use knickers, vest and a jacket called «steglatrøye». Men from inner Sogn used a light colored jacket, while those from outer Sogn wore a dark jacket. They changed the style around 1860 to a tight, fitted jacket and trousers. But some men continued to wear the jacket called «steglatrøya» up until the turn of the century.

The jacket is made of white frieze with black velvet trim. The jacket, called «steglatrøya», has gores in back. It has shoulder edges. The knickers are made of dark wool material. They have a buckle and a row of silver buttons on the outside of each knee. The vest is made of red wool material with black velvet trim. It has a stand-up collar and two rows of silver buttons. A white linen shirt, with whitework or black stitch embroidery around the collar and cuffs of the sleeves is worn.

A hat made of red wool material with black velvet trim is part of the bunad, along with white, knitted wool stockings and black shoes with buckles. The bunad silver consists of a neck button with dangles and button cufflinks for the shirt, and all the silver buttons for the vest and the trousers.

Woman's bunad from Jølster

Olina Fossheim began creating the new Jølster bunad in 1914. For generations, traditional costumes were worn both for formal and daily use. Antique costume materials were preserved and old women passed on information about the bunad design. The traditional costume had a black or blue skirt, a short black jacket, a stripe patterned apron, a hat with white lacework, stiffened loose collar and a shoulder scarf that they wore to church. The bunad became known outside Jølster, at a convention in 1922. Many years passed until it developed into the design of today. It was difficult to get the right materials in the right colors. The Sunnfjord bunad can have various belts and apron patterns and be made in different colors. The costume pictured is one version of the woman's bunad from Jølster.

The skirt is made of black or dark blue wool material with a red hem and white cross-stitch embroidery above the hem. It is pleated, with a kick-pleat in back. A red colored jacket, made of wool, with dark blue, green, white and yellow trim is part of the bunad. It is open in front, with a few concealed hooks right above the waistline. There is a hook on each cuff of the sleeves. It has a red or dark blue bodice, with narrow trim in green or red and also a woven band. The bodice closes with hooks, above the waistline. On each side of the opening in front, there is a piece of decorative band, called «eyelet cloths». The blouse is made of white linen with whitework around the collar, on each side of the front placket and on the cuffs of the sleeves. It has a home-woven, half-woolen apron in different striped patterns. (The apron shown in the photo is called «randa-apron».) The hat for this model is made of black or dark blue cloth, with white stiffened lace work around the edge and two patterned streamers hanging down in back. The girls' hat, shown in the photos, has a red silk edge, while the women use a black silk edge. A belt made of red cloth with goldfilled ornaments and a buckle in front is part of this bunad, also gilded ornaments on the streamer hanging down in front. Woven ties can be used for the apron instead of the silver belt. Black stockings and black shoes are part of the costume. The bunad silver consists of a neck button with dangles, button cufflinks and one or two brooches, the gilded ornaments on the belt and its streamer and the belt buckle.

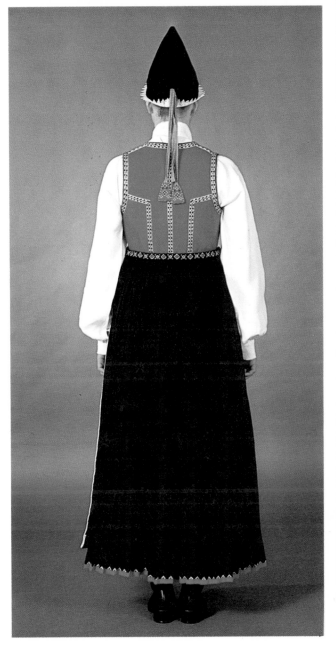

Man's bunad from Sunnfjord

This bunad was designed by the Young People's Society of Sunnfjord in 1964. It was copied after antique costumes from the Sunnfjord Folk Museum. The jacket was copied after an antique frieze jacket with embroideries, and the vest was copied after a short, green vest made of wool material. Antique pants, called «blokabukse», were the model for the trousers. A similar costume was designed in 1960 by Gunvor Trætteberg in cooperation with Heimen, «the Home», in Oslo. For this version, they copied an antique jacket from Sunnfjord, now to be found at the Historical Museum in Bergen.

The jacket is made of red frieze, with green wool yarn embroidered trim. It has a stand-up collar and a single row of brass buttons, and a pair of black frieze knickers with a flap in front. There is a row of brass buttons on the outside of each knee. The vest is made of green wool material with a high, stand-up collar and two rows of buttons (double buttoned). A white linen shirt with whitework around the high collar and the cuffs of the sleeves in part of the costume. A knitted hat with a napped trim may be worn. The belt is made of white linen cloth with cross-stitch embroidery in a variety of colors. It closes with a brass buckle. Solid white, rose patterned or checked stockings, held up by garters made in a variety of colors, and black shoes with buckles are part of the costume. The bunad silver consists of a neck button with dangles, and button cuff-links for the shirt. The belt buckle and buttons are made of brass.

Woman's bunad from Nordfjord

The very first woman's bunad from Nordfjord was designed by Mina Rye and it was displayed in public for the first time at a fair in Sandane in 1927. In 1947, the Young People's Society from Firda registered the Nordfjord bunads, made in the 1920s, for a redesign. But after they had gathered all the information about the costume, very little had to be changed. Black, blue, red and green bodices with oblique seams on each side of the center seam in back had been in use in the district. The pattern on the apron and on the decorative edge-bands might be different from district to district. But the skirt's design appears to have been the same all over Nordfjord.

The skirt is made of black, all-wool material with a woven band around the hem. It is pleated. The bodice is made of black or green wool material with woven trimming. It has a chainlaced bodice. The blouse is made of white linen with whitework «krunekret», around the collar and cuffs of the sleeves. The blouse may have either a stand-up or a turn-down collar. Two different wool aprons can be used with this bunad. The photo shows an apron called «fota-apron», the other type is called «krune-apron». The apron can have either woven or embroidered ties. Either a kerchief or a hat may be worn. The kerchief has drawn work, embroidery and fringe, and it is tied on the left side in back. It has a hat made of black silk brocade with a black silk trim and black silk bands, tied in a bow in back. A little edge of the white linen head scarf shows underneath. Women wear a solid black silk hat, while young girls wear a patterned silk hat. Black stockings and black shoes are part of the costume. The bunad silver consists of a neck pin with dangles, button cufflinks and a brooch for the blouse, and silver eyelets and silver chain for the bodice.

Man's bunad from Nordfjord

This bunad was in use in the 1920s. A branch of the Young People's Society in Firda started a study of antique men's costumes in 1947. There was no reason to change the 1920 bunad. Joachim Frich did three drawings of men's bunads in 1845. One of the drawings shows exactly the same costume as is worn today, with the same jacket and knickers. In the last part of the 19th C the man's costume from Nordfjord used to have a short, tight, fitted jacket design. It can be used with the current bunad.

The jacket is made of blue colored cloth. It is hip length in back, with an oblique cut up to the waistline in front. It has a row of silver buttons on each side of the opening in front, but they are not buttoned. The jacket has one button on the outside of each sleeve and two buttons in back. It has a stand-up collar, turn-down lapels and pocket flaps. A short designed jacket can be used.

The knickers are made of the same material as the jacket with a flap in front, a buckle and a row of silver buttons on the outside of each knee. The vest is made of green wool material with black trim, it closes with a row of silver buttons. It has a square shaped neckline, but no collar. A vest with a V-shaped neckline and a stand-up collar can also be used. The white chiffon cloth shirt can have whitework around the collar and on cuffs of the sleeves.

Blue and white, or just plain with pattern knitted stockings, with colorful garters and black shoes with buckles are part of the costume. The bunad silver consists of a neck button with dangles and button cufflinks for the blouse, and all the buttons for the jacket, vest and knickers.

MØRE AND ROMSDAL

In Møre and Romsdal we distinguish between the bunads in Sunnmøre, Romsdal and Nordmøre. None of the bunads of today is a direct continuation of a folk costume tradition. But we have old, preserved costume material, such as folk costume pictures from the last century from all three districts. The bunads of today are partly based on this material.

The Sunnmøre woman's bunad came into use early in this century. In the 1920s it was revised, and the first Ørskog bunad was displayed in 1927 as a result of this bunad revision. Today the Sunnmøre bunad for women has 10 variations, with different embroideries. The men's bunad, as used in Sunnmøre today, builds on the last folk costume type worn in this district.

In Romsdal it was Mali Furunes at the Romsdal Museum who spearheaded the bunad work since the 1920s. She was the folk dance instructor, thus a colleague and friend of Klara Semb. Today the Romsdal woman's bunad appears in several variations. There are two men's bunads, one appearing in the 1920s, with the «gray vest» as the model, while the other was designed in the 1940s, based on a watercolor by the artist J.F.L. Dreier, showing a Romsdal man in a red jacket.

The work on a local woman's bunad for Nordmøre was initiated in 1937. It was first worn right after the war. The man's bunad for Nordmøre was designed by «Heimen» in Oslo in the 1920s.

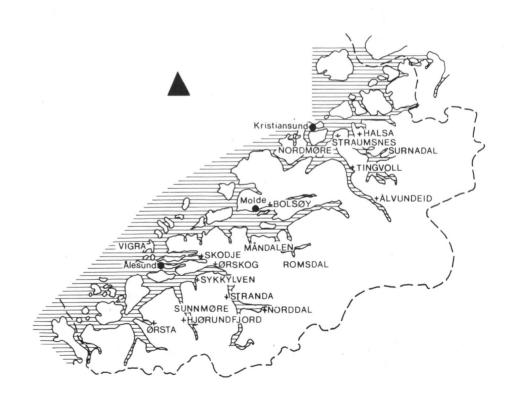

«A Surendal man with his girlfriend». Johannes Senn: «Norwegian National Costumes». Copenhagen 1812—15.

Woman's bunad from Sunnmøre — The Ørskog bunad

Sunnmøre Husflidslag and the Young People's Society recreated the Sunnmørs-bunad in the 1920s. It was copied after antique costumes. It was photographed in Hulda Garborg's book «Norwegian Costumes», written in 1917. Ragnhild Vogt Svendsen designed the Sunnmørs-bunad which was on display in Ålesund in 1927. That was the very first Ørskogbunad. The Sunnmørbunad came in different variations with embroidery from different districts. The embroidery was copied from a bodice and an apron belonging to the same costume. The antique skirts used to be made in solid colors. They were either pleated or tucked. The women from Sunnmøre used a high hat in the mid 18th C; in the last century they used a hat called «kolle-hat», which is the same type of hat that is worn today. A kerchief is used with the formal costume. A black embroidered linen scarf was used to copy the women's kerchief. The same kind of kerchief is used for young girls, except for the colorful embroidery. The embroidered purse was used in Sunnmøre in this century after the antique costume was no longer used.

There are ten different Sunnmørbunads. The bunad described here is the Ørskogbunad. It is made of black or blue woolen material; it can have a woven hem. The skirt is either pleated or tucked. It has a bodice made of the same cloth as the skirt with thin red trim and with colorful wool yarn embroidery in front and back. It closes with three hooks right above the waistline in front and one hook at the bodice neckline. The blouse is made of white linen with whitework around the collar and cuffs of the sleeves. It has an apron made of the same material as the skirt and with the same embroidery. The length is the same as the skirt. Either kerchief or hat can be worn. The design of the hat is based on a more certain tradition than the kerchief. The hat is called «kolle-hat», and is made of the same material as the skirt. The woman's kerchief is made of white linen with black stitch embroidery, while the girl's kerchief has colorful embroidery. Otherwise it is the same style. It is fastened to the head with silk ties with decorative stitches. It has a purse made of the same material as the skirt, with red trim and colorful embroidery. The purse closing is made of silver or brass. Red or black stockings and black shoes are part of the costume. A medium long cape made of the same material as the rest of the costume is used for the outdoors. It has a high collar and red lining and it closes around the neck with a silver buckle. The bunad silver consists of the «Sunnmør button», and neck button with dangles. A little round brooch with dangles and the silver buckle for the cape, and a silver or brass purse closing.

Woman's bunad from Vigra

Two of the Sunnmør bunads came from southern and outer Sunnmøre. The only detail that separates the Vigra bunad from the rest of the Sunnmør bunads is the square shaped neckline. Otherwise the blouse and the skirt are the same for all Sunnmør bunads. From old pictures one can see that the antique costume had the square shaped neckline edged with a wide patterned band. For the antique bodice they used flower patterned silk bands around the edges. The apron is copied after an apron from Vigra believed to be 250 years old. It got its present design in the 1930s.

The skirt is made of black or blue woolen cloth, and is finely pleated. The bodice is made of orange colored wool damask with a wide trim around the neckline made of the same material as the skirt and with a colorful embroidery. It has concealed hooks in front. The blouse is made of white linen with whitework around the collar and cuffs of the sleeves. The apron is made of home woven half-wool in a colorful striped pattern. It has a colorful flower embroidery in wool yarn between the striped pattern.

The hat called «kolle-hat» or a kerchief can be used. The purse is made of the same material as the skirt with a colorful embroidery and a brass closing. Black or red stockings and black shoes are part of the costume. A medium long cape made of the same material as the skirt is used for the outdoors. It has a high collar and closes with a silver buckle. The buand silver consists of a neck button and a brooch and also button cufflinks for the blouse.

Man's bunad from Sunnmøre

Around the last part of the 18th C, the men from Sunnmøre wore a medium long white frieze jacket over a shorter jacket. In the area of the fjords, the men wore leather knickers but nearer the coast they used knickers made of frieze. The bunad got a new formal jacket in the 1840s. It was short in front with tail back. A vest was used underneath. The costume shown in the photos was copied after the short, tight-fitted jacket from the last part of the last century called «rund-trøye-kleda». It came into use as a bunad in the 1920s.

The jacket is made of black wool. It has stand-up collar and turn-down lapels with a row of silver, brass or pewter buttons on each side of the opening in front. They cannot be buttoned. The knickers are made of the same material as the jacket with a flap in front. It has a buckle and a row of buttons by the outside of each knee. A red vest made of wool material, no collar, but with two rows of silver buttons in front.

The shirt is made of white linen with whitework around the collar and cuffs of the sleeves. Garters made in a variety of colors are tied underneath the cuffs so only the ends and tassels show. White pattern knitted stockings and black shoes are part of the costume. The bunad silver consists of a neck button and button cufflinks for the blouse. All the buttons for the knickers, jacket and the vest, can be made of either silver, brass or pewter.

189

Woman's bunad from Romsdal —
The Bolsøy bunad

The formal costume for Romsdal was designed between 1920—1930. The traditional plain jumper was worn by women in different districts in Romsdal, for into this century. But it was not considered fancy enough for a formal costume. The formal Romsdal bunad was copied from an embroidered bodice with peplum dated about the last part of the 18th C to the first part of the 19th C. The antique bodices can be found at the Romsdals Museum. There are four variations of the woman's bunad from Romsdal. The bunad described here is the Bolsøy costume. The bodice was copied after an antique bodice from the Romsdal Museum, and the skirt was copied from an antique underskirt from Bolsøy.

The skirt is made of blue woolen cloth with a colorful flower pattern border embroidery. It is pleated with a red hem. The bodice is made of red wool with flower pattern embroidery in front and back. It has a peplum and closes in front with concealed hooks. The blouse is made of white linen with whitework around the collar on part of the shoulders and on cuffs of the sleeves. The hat is tucked, made of the same material as the skirt and with wool yarn embroidery in back. It also has lacework around the front edge. The purse is made of the same material as the bodice, with colorful flower pattern embroidery and a brass closing. Red stockings and shoes are part of the costume. A cape, made of the same material as the skirt, is used for the outdoors. The bunad silver consists of a neck button (Romsdal button). The Romsdal brooch and button cufflinks for the blouse. The jewelry was made after the Second World War.

Man's bunad from Romsdal

This man's bunad was designed in the 1920s after an antique costume from Romsdal. We do not know today which pieces of clothing were copied. A publication about the Romsdal bunad from 1926 included material on the half-length jacket called «Spelfrakken». It was seen in a painting from Molde, done about 1778, and was worn in different districts as late as the 1880s. The vest is made of the same material as the skirt copied from a woman's bunad from Måndalen.

The jacket is made of grey woolen material with green trim and button-holes. It is half-long with a fold and a split in back, a row of silver buttons on each side of the opening in front, stand-up collar and the lapels are held down with silver buttons. The pocket flaps have a green fringe and green trim made of wool, and three silver buttons. It has knickers made of blue woolen material with a flap in front, a buckle and a row of silver buttons on the outside of each knee. The shirt is made of white linen with whitework around the collar and cuffs of the sleeves. It also has a plaid wool vest with a row of silver buttons on each side of the opening in front. It has a grey knitted hat with a green napped trim. The colorful garters are tied under the knickers cuffs so only the ends can be seen. The bunad silver consists of a neck button (Romsdal button) and button cufflinks for the shirt, and all the silver buttons for the knickers, jacket and vest. The silver buttons can be made in filigree.

Woman's bunad from Nordmøre

Nordmøre Bondekvinnelag took the initiative to redesign the woman's bunad from Nordmøre in 1937. The bunad was completed in 1939, but it was lost in a fire the following year, and no new bunad was made until after the Second World War. It was copied after antique garments from different districts in Nordmøre. It was easy to find appropriate blouses for the new bunad. The whitework from Nordmøre is famous. Antique bodices from Straumsnes, Hasla, Tingvoll, Ålvundeid and Surnadal were used to copy the new bodice. All the antique skirts were finely pleated around the waistline; they were made of green, blue, black or brown woolen material. The apron shown in the photos is an exact copy of an antique apron from Romfo in Surnadalen.

The Nordmøre bunad can be made in different color combinations with bodice made of either damask or brocade material. The skirt is made of black, brown, blue or green wool. It is finely pleated. It has a bodice made of damask or brocade in colors that match the skirt; it has decorative silver bands around the bodice opening and neckline in front.

The blouse is made of white linen with whitework around the collar, the front pocket and cuffs of the sleeves. The apron is made of wool or linen in red, green or brown. Two different silk aprons can also be used. The hat («piklua») has a pointed shape. It is made of black, blue or brown velvet, with a colorful embroidered border around the front edge. The color of the hat should go with the color of the rest of the bunad. The embroidery on the borders can vary. The hat has black ties. It has a belt made of the same material as the skirt with silver ornaments or a colorful Nordmøre embroidery. It closes in front with a silver buckle. The purse is made of the same material as the skirt. It has a colorful wool yarn embroidery or trim made of the same material as the bodice. The closing is made of brass or silver. Black or red stockings and black shoes are part of the costume. The bunad silver consists of a buckle and the ornaments on the belt, and the blouse closes at the neckline with a Nordmøre brooch. An Agnus Dei pendant can be worn in a chain around the neck.

Man's bunad from Nordmøre

This bunad was designed by Anna Johannesen at Heimen (the Home) in 1922. The publication «For Country and City» of 1922, said that the costume was copied after old pictures and in consultation with people from Nordmøre. That is the best information given about the antique costume. The bunad shown in the photos was made by a tailor from Nordmøre.

The jacket is made of brown wool material with dark red applique on the stand-up collar and in back. The cuffs are slit and both the button holes and the slit have red trim. The jacket has two rows of buttons on each side in front, one button on each pocket flap and two buttons in back. The knickers are made of the same material as the jacket, with dark red applique embroidery and button holes. It has a flap in front, buckle and a row of buttons on the outside of each knee. The vest is made of blue, double-shuttle wool material with a colorful embroidery in front. It does not have a collar but a single row of buttons and black trim.

The shirt is made of white linen with whitework around the collar and cuffs of the sleeves. A neck scarf can also be used. Blue stockings with colorful garters and black shoes are part of the costume. The bunad silver consists of a neck brooch with dangles and button cufflinks for the shirt. The buttons for the jacket, vest and knickers, can be made of either silver or pewter.

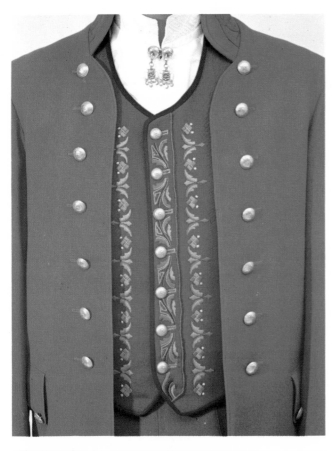

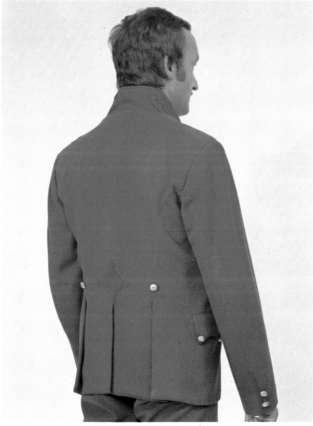

197

TRØNDELAG

«**B**ut all the bunads have long since gone up there. . .», Hulda Garborg wrote about Trøndelag in 1917. She excluded, however, the traditional Røros costumes still in use in her time. It was only on more special occasions the old costumes were worn earlier in this century, yet they have never been completely stored away. The Røros bunads are in many ways similar to the folk costumes, one still distinguishes married from unmarried. In addition, the Røros women wear the dark jacket as a festive garment for the bunad, as it was used in the last century.

The Trøndelag Lapps keep alive the folk costume tradition. We distinguish between the Røros-Lapp costumes and those used in Nord-Trøndelag. The Trønder Lapp costumes belong to the Lapp costumes on the Swedish side of the border, and not to the Norwegian bunads in Trøndelag. We are, therefore, not going to review the Lapp costumes here.

Thanks to the Trøndelag artist, J.F. Dreier, who drew the folk costumes from about 1800, we know something about the folk costumes in Trøndelag at the end of the 18th C. As Dreier depicted them, the women had jackets and aprons on top of solid-colored or striped skirts. The men had narrow knee-pants and long jackets.

Yet, when in the 1920s efforts were made to design a special bunad for Trøndelag they no longer had any folk costume to build on. The models of the «Trønder-bunad» for women are, therefore, based on scattered folk costume material and Dreier's drawings. The bunad was designed to be a festive bunad for *all* Trøndelag people. Gradually, however, several bunads for various areas of the district have appeared. In 1938 Hjørdis Halmøy Floan designed the «Nord-Trøndelag bunad» and later a man's bunad for Nord-Trøndelag. After the war Oppdal, Meldal, Rennebu and Namdalen have all got their own women's bunads. In the beginning of the 1950s came a man's costume for Sør-Trøndelag, and right now the finishing touches are put on a new Selbu bunad for women.

«A man from Hitterver with his wife». Johannes Senn: «Norwegian National Costumes». Copenhagen 1812—15.

Woman's bunad from Røros

The traditional Røros bunad was never out of use, so we know exactly how it was used. There were certain rules about who could use which costume and how it should be worn. It was up to the individual person to choose colors and material for the costume, which is also the case today. The woman's hat is different from the girl's hat. The women use a black hat («øre-hatt»). The black bow in back is fastened to the ties. The girls use a brown hat daily and an embroidered hat for formal occasions; it had a red bow and red patterned ties. The colors and patterns in the skirt, apron and shoulder scarf can vary, depending on one's ability to mix colors and materials.

The skirt is made of plaid or striped wool material; it is folded with a kick-pleat in back. It has a black or blue jacket made of cloth. This jacket is called «spensel» — it has wide puffed sleeves that narrow toward the cuffs, a peplum and also a belt. Under the jacket is worn a white neck-scarf, and only a narrow edge of it can be seen under the shoulder scarf. The hat is made of black silk with a black bow in back and black ties (Hukku-band); it can be made of fine pattern woven silk, but should always be black for women. The hat has a particular fine cut that can better be seen on the girl's hat on page 203. The apron can be made of plaid flower patterned or solid colored silk or wool material. A flower patterned wool scarf or silk with a fings is worn over the shoulders and tied in front. The scarf in the photos was an heirloom. The purse is made of solid colored wool with flower patterend embroidery and it has a brass closing. White, blue, red or black stockings and black shoes are part of the costume. A blue silk damask cape with a fur collar is used for the outdoors.

Young girls' bunads from Røros

There is a difference between a married woman's and an unmarried woman's bunad from Røros. In the photos, two young girls show two different bunad designs. They are both used as bunads today. They are older and younger versions of the costumes from the last century. Like the woman's bunad, the girl's costume can vary in different materials, colors and patterns for the skirt, jacket, apron and shoulder scarf. But the hat maintains the same style and color. The girl's and woman's hats differ. The embroidered hat with a red bow was used for formal occasions. The brown hat with a dark brown trim and a red bow was used for everyday wear. A solid red or patterned neck bow was also worn.

The older of the costumes pictured here has a black jacket with a peplum, and a plaid or striped skirt. The tailored jacket with skirt made of the same material is of a more recent date, it was designed in the last part of the 19th C. The jacket is V-shaped in front, and flared in the back. The skirt is finely pleated in back to give the appearance of a bustle. Black, blue, red or white stockings and black shoes are part of the costume.

Man's bunad from Røros

The man's bunad from Røros was copied after the married man's costume from the last century. Antique costumes are preserved since the costume never was out of use. In this century, some men used the costume for church and for formal occasions. Røros Young People's Society members wore it for their Røros evenings in the 1920s. And it has been used through the years at cultural gatherings. Single men from Røros used a short, tightly fitted jacket (rundtrøye-kleda) and trousers in the last part of the last century, and they also wore a red hat. Today, the red hat is the only status symbol of being a single man. The married man's hip-length jacket and knickers are used as a model for the bunad of today.

The jacket is made of black or dark blue frieze or cloth, with a row of brass buttons on each side of the opening in front, a stand-up collar and small, turn-back lapels. It has brass buttons on the pocket flaps and to mark the joinings in back. The knickers are made of the same material as the jacket, they have a flap in front, a buckle and a row of brass buttons on the outside of each knee. On the outside of the lower leg, underneath the buckle, a little scalloped piece of the same material as the knickers, hangs down. The vest can be made of different materials and colors, in checked, striped or other patterns. The vest shown in the photos is made of solid color, pattern-woven brocade, with two rows of brass buttons in front. It buttons up to the neckline.

There is no particular shirt made for this bunad, but it is usually worn with a white shirt of antique design. A loose shirtfront can also be used. A patterned, silk neck scarf, tied in a bow is worn. The hat for married men is knitted in dark gray or black with a red trim. Single men wear a red knitted hat. White or blue stockings and black shoes with metal buckles are part of the costume.

The Trønder bunad

In 1923 three teachers, Kaspara Kyllingstad, Ingeborg Krogstad and Ragna Rytter, introduced the new formal bunad for the entire Trøndelag district. It was the result of tree years of research. They were not able to find a complete costume, but antique photos and garments convinced them that the new bunad should be based on the 19th C rococco style which was popular in Trøndelag. The bodice was made of finer, imported material. The skirt was made of solid colored or striped pattern material. Embroidered hats and purses were used. The first embroidered hats were copied after flower embroidered hats from Singsås. The white linen head scarf, called «bridal linen», came from Selbu.

The Trønder bunad can be made of red, blue or green all-wool material with a red hem on the blue and green skirts and a green hem on the red skirt. It has a plain front panel and is finely pleated in back to give the appearance of a bustle. The bodice is made of wool damask in the same background color as the skirt, with a scalloped peplum, decorated with red trim on the blue and green vest, and green trim on the red vest. It closes with two or three hooks above the waistline and one at the neckline. The blouse is made of white linen with whitework on part of the shoulders and around the collar and cuffs of the sleeves. The apron is made of linen damask in dark gray and white, or green and white pattern. It has a hat made of black silk with colorful embroidery; four different patterns can be used. A white linen head scarf with drawn work can also be worn. It is fastened to a red colored roll of a padding. The purse has colorful embroidery. There are four different patterns to choose from, and it has a brass closing. Red stockings for the blue and green bunad and green stockings for the red bunad and black shoes with silver buckles are part of the costume. The bunad silver consists of a brooch with dangles, and a larger brooch or an Agnus Dei pendant on a silver chain. The hooks on the bodice and the button cufflinks are made of silver. A blue wool damask cape can be used for the outdoors.

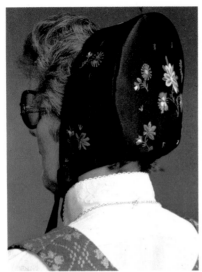

Woman's bunad from Rennebu

The Rennebu bunad was designed in the beginning of the 1950s by Kjellaug Tverdahl. Registered costume material from Rennebu was used. The bodice was copied after a bodice with a printed pattern from Hoset. Printed materials were common in Trøndelag in the last century. Besides dyeing the cloth, they also printed beautiful patterns. The bunad silver was copied from antique silver from Rennebu.

The skirt is made of black, blue, green or red wool material. It has a plain panel in front and is finely pleated in back to give the appearance of a bustle. Underneath the skirt a roll of padding is tied around the hips. The bodice is made of either green or red wool with a printed pattern in black. It has a split in back, it closes with concealed hooks and a silver buckle at the waistline. The blouse is made of white linen with whitework around the collar and cuffs of the sleeves. The apron can be made of black silk damask or it can have a white apron with a woven or embroidered pattern and ties. Three different hats are designed for this bunad, a young girl's hat, young married woman's and married woman's hats. The one shown in the photos is a woman's hat. It is made of black velvet with lacework around the front edge, and black ties. It can also be made of black silk. A cape is used for the outdoors, and is made of blue or black wool with red linen or wool lining with a printed pattern. It also has a hood and closes at the neckline with a silver buckle. Black or red stockings and black shoes are part of the costume. The bunad silver consists of button cufflinks, two brooches for the blouse, a silver buckle for the bodice and one for the cape. The buckles and buttons were copied after antique silver from Rennebu.

Man's bunad from Sør-Trøndelag

This bunad was designed in the first part of the 1950s for the Young Farm People's Society in Nidaros. It is copied after an antique man's costume from Ålen, from about 1850. This was the last homemade costume design, before ready-made clothing came into use around the turn of the century. The same bunad design is used today.

The jacket is made of dark blue frieze, with a stand-up collar and a row of silver buttons on each side of the opening in front. The knickers are made of the same material as the jacket. It has a flap in front, a buckle and a row of silver buttons on the outside of the knees. It has a home woven vest in wool and linen material with a striped pattern, stand-up collar and double rows of silver buttons in front. The shirt is made of white linen with whitework around the collar and the cuffs of the sleeves. White patterned knitted stockings, with colorful garters tied around the knees, and black shoes with buckles are part of the costume. The bunad silver consists of a neck button with dangles, and all the buttons for the jacket, knickers, and vest. The silver buttons on the jacket and vest are the same, but the buttons on the knickers are different. All the buttons are copied after an old costume from Ålen.

211

Woman's bunad from Namdalen

The idea of a special bunad for Namdalen surfaced in 1934, but the final result was completed in the middle of the 1950s. Kaia Severeide from Rørvik designed it. The antique skirt and the silver can be found at Paul Woxeng's Museum in Vikna. The antique skirt was green with a printed pattern. The pattern was copied from an original print block from the old Trønder dye houses. Besides dyeing materials, they also did printing. Sverresborg Museum had many print blocks with different patterns. The copy for the bodice came from Overhalla, the blouse copy came from Grong and the hat's copy came from Nordli. As long as the colors are in tone with the rest of the bunad, the silk scarf can vary.

The skirt is made of green wool material with a printed pattern in black, with a red hem. It is pleated. The vest is made of red silk damask with a peplum, it closes with two silver buckles above the waistline and a hook at the neckline. The blouse is made of white linen with whitework around the collar and the cuffs of the sleeves. It has a tucked black velvet hat, with black silk ties. A black silk scarf is the most common, but it can vary in patterns and colors. The purse is made of the same material as the bodice and black velvet. The purse closing is made of brass. The bunad silver consists of button cufflinks, a little neck brooch, a larger brooch and silver buckles for the blouse. The silver is copied from a pewter pattern found at Woxeng's Museum in Vikna.

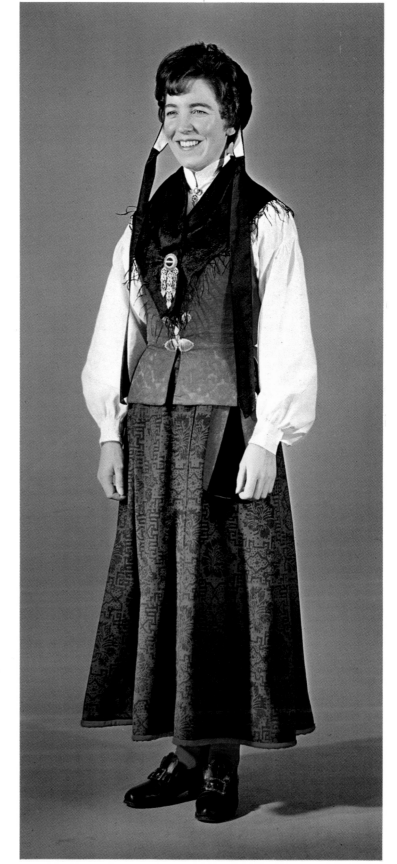

NORDLAND

The folk costume traditions in the district of Nordland are all tied in with the Lapp areas, as far as we know. The Lapp costumes in the southern parts of the district are connected with the South-Lapp costumes in Nord-Trøndelag and corresponding areas on the Swedish side of the border, while, for instance, the Tysfjord costumes belong to the cultural sphere of the Lule Lapps.

The work on the Norwegian bunads in the district of Nordland was initiated in the 1920s and was intimately connected with the liberal youth work, the folk dance and the folk high schools. In 1926 the Nordland Youth Society named a bunad committee which was to search for old costume garments which could serve as a basis for a woman's bunad for Nordland. The work was finished in 1928. The first man's bunad, named «Man's Bunad for Nordland», was completed already in 1923/24. Originally it was designed in Troms, and as it essentially builds on costume material from Troms, we have decided to place it under the district of Troms. The Nordland bunad for men and women, was meant to be the festive costumes for all of North Norway.

In the 1930s, Bergliot Wicklund began to work on the Hamarøy bunad, with an old, embroidered skirt from Ulvsvåg, Hamarøy, as the starting point. At Vestvågøy the «Husflidslaget» planned a special Hols bunad. The artist, Edvarda Lie, designed a flower motif for the bunad which was named the «Lofoten bunad» and appeared in 1948.

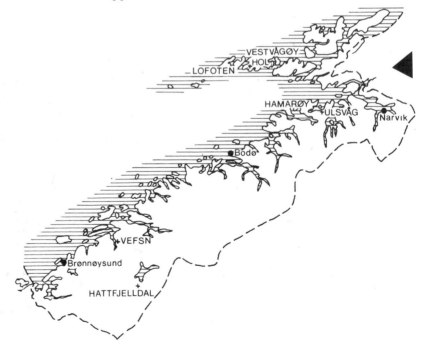

People on way to church at Nordlandet, Værøy. Theodor Kittelsen: «From Lofoten», Christiania 1890.

The Nordland bunad or «Vefsnbunad»

The first Nordland bunad was shown at a Hålogaland Young People's Society meeting in Leir-fjord in 1928. It was designed by a bunad group within the Society. It was meant to be a formal costume for all of North-Norway. The bunad is also called «Vefsnbunad» because the idea came from Vefsn. In the last century, the women from Nordland wore plain dresses, but they wore silk dresses for formal occasions. When they designed the bunad, they wanted to get away from imported silk and use only Norwegian fabrics. The bunad's cut was copied from a wedding dress from Ravassåsen in Vefsn. The embroidery was copied from a plastron and a purse from Røyten in Vefsn, and the apron's pattern came from Hattfjelldal. The hat was copied after the «black hat» that was used in the last part of the 19th C, but now it has the same color as the rest of the bunad.

The Nordland bunad can be made in either blue or green. The skirt is made of either blue or green cloth with a colorful border of embroidery in wool yarn. It is pleated in front and more finely pleated in back. The bodice is made of the same material as the skirt, with flower embroidery in front and back. It closes in front with two silver hooks and a concealed hook at the neckline. The blouse is made of white linen with whitework around the collar and the cuffs of the sleeves. It has a plaid cotton apron, and a shawl made of the same material as the apron, and with a fringe. The hat is made of the same material as the rest of the bunad, it is tucked with lacework around the front edge. It has a purse made of the same material as the skirt and with the same flower embroidery. Black or white shoes are part of the costume. The bunad silver consists of silver buckles for the bodice and one or two brooches and button cufflinks for the blouse. The jewelry is designed especially for this bunad.

Woman's bunad from Hamarøy

The Hamarøy bunad was copied after a brown, flower patterned skirt from Ulvsvåg and a green damask jacket from Bodø, from about 1790. Bergliot Wicklund found these antique costumes at the Nordenfjeldske Art and Industry Museum in Trondheim. The skirt is to be found at Nordland District Museum. It has been made in different variations through the years. The bunad worn today has a brown skirt with flower patterned embroidery copied after an antique skirt from Ulvsvåg. And it also has a red embroidered bodice with a peplum.

The brown woolen skirt has a red colored wool hem. It has a wool yarn embroidered border in different flower patterns. The skirt is pleated. It has a red wool bodice with a peplum. Details from the embroidered skirt border are used as a copy for the embroidery in back and on each side of the opening in front. The bodice closes in front with concealed hooks.

It has a white linen blouse with whitework around the collar and cuffs of the sleeves. The hat is made of the same materials as the skirt, with embroidery on the front piece and in back. It has a purse, also made of the same material as the skirt and with the same embroidery, and a silver closing. Black shoes and black stockings are part of the costume. The bunad silver consists of button cufflinks, a little neck brooch and a bigger brooch, and a silver purse closing.

TROMS

In Troms, aside from the Lapp areas, we do not know about any folk costume tradition. The Lapp costumes are, in some places, still in everyday use, and on festive occasions. In other parts of Troms, we find a renewed interest in the usage of Lapp costumes, no longer in use. Here one has a secure foundation for the reconstruction work as old garments and pictures are preserved. There are still many people alive who wore these costumes.

The liberal youth movement became interested in designing their own bunad. In the 1920s, began the collection of old garments which could be the starting point for bunads both for men and women. Material was collected both in Troms and Nordland, and the idea was that the bunads were to become festive costumes for the whole of North Norway. The first «Nordland bunad» for men was done by a tailor at Harstad. We have, therefore, elected to place that bunad under the district of Troms.

Just before the war, the Målselv Husflidslag began to work on a special bunad for Bardu and Målselv, but not until after the war the work really progressed. The bunad has the same shape as the women's bunads in Gudbrandsdalen. Its embroidery was designed by Halfdan Arneberg who was inspired by an embroidered cap, probably from Oppdal. The models of the man's bunad for Bardu and Målselv are men's costumes from Gudbrandsdalen and Østerdalen. The man's bunad was presented in 1967. It is designed by a committee with members from the Bardu Township Council, Målselv Mållag and Målselv Husflidslag.

In 1973 appeared the new woman's bunad for Troms, the «Troms bunad», designed by Troms Ungdomsfylking and BUL, Tromsø, based on old garments and pictures from various areas in Troms.

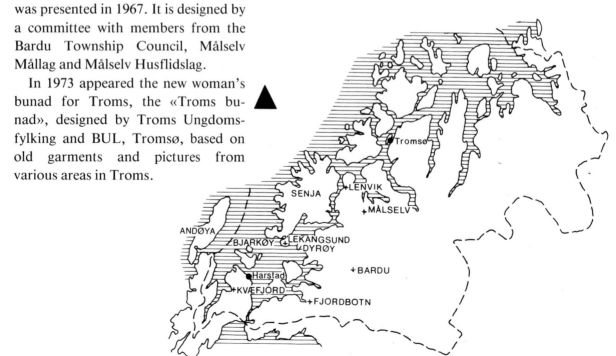

«From Lake Jæger». Photo: Lindahl, 1890. (University Library).

The Troms bunad

The Troms bunad was on display for the first time at the Troms Ungdomsfylking meeting in Senjahopen in 1973. Since 1967, Troms Ungdomsfylking and BUL in Tromsø had been searching for antique clothing and pictures, to form the basis of a woman's costume for the whole district. The skirt's cut was copied from a wedding dress from Lekangsund in Senja. And the material for the skirt was copied after an antique material from Anna Grostøl's collection of home woven materials in Troms, now at Tromsø Museum. An old hat from Kvæfjord was used as a copy for the new hat, while the apron was inspired by an apron from an antique photo from Dyrøy. A goldsmith from Tromsø designed the bunad silver after silver buttons from Tromsø Museum.

The skirt is made of black and yellow blend, all wool with black stripes. It has black velvet bands above the hem. The skirt is pleated in front and more finely pleated in back to give the appearance of a bustle, and a concealed pocket on one side. The bodice is made of red or yellow patterned brocade, it reaches just above the waistline in front with a peplum in back, and it buttons with silver buttons in front. It has a white linen blouse with whitework around the collar and cuffs of the sleeves. The apron is made of cotton with black and white striped pattern. Two different hats can be used with this bunad, both made of black silk with white lace work around the front edge. A bow or a scarf in checked taffeta or gloria yarn is worn inside the neckline. Black stockings and black shoes are part of the costume. A black all-wool cape is used for the outdoors. The bunad silver consists of buttons for the vest, button cufflinks and a brooch for the blouse, and also a little brooch for the neck bow.

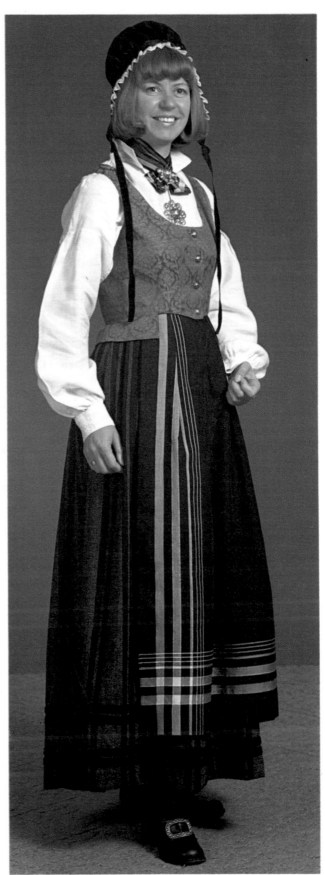

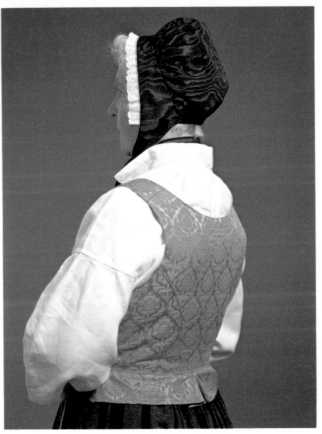

Man's bunad from Nordland

The first Nordland bunad for men was made as a wedding costume for Johs. Eidnes by the tailor Cornelius Jakobsen from Harstad, about 1923—1924. J. Eidnes was active in youth work, and a part of his work was to collect background material for a man's bunad for Northern Norway. The model for this bunad comes from different places in Nordland and Troms districts, such as: Lofoten, Dunderlandsdalen, Vefsn, Andøya, Lenvik and Kvæfjord.

It has a black jacket made of cloth, with a stand-up collar and turn-back lapels. There is a row of silver buttons on each side of the opening in front and on the cuffs of the sleeves. The knickers are made of black cloth with a flap in front. It has a buckle and a row of silver buttons at the outside of the knees. The vest can be made of red, blue or checkered wool material, or of flower pattern brocade as in the photo. It has a row of silver buttons on each side of the opening in front and turn-back lapels. The shirt is made of white linen or cotton cloth, with a stand-up collar. A patterned neck scarf in a variety of colors is tied in a bow in front. It has blue stockings with white spots and patterned garters. Black shoes with buckles are part of the costume. The bunad silver consists of all the silver buttons for the jacket, vest and knickers.

FINNMARK

In the Lapp areas of Finnmark, many people still wear Lapp garments for everyday use and on festive occasions. Here we face a viable folk costume tradition, even if most use «Norwegian» clothes in addition to, or instead of, Lapp garments. The Lapp costumes in the townships of Sør-Varanger, Nesseby, Tana/Karasjok/Porsanger and Kautokeino are different. But the Lapp costume areas are larger than one single township, and they cross township, district and national borders. The Lapp costumes are not included in this volume because they belong to a different cultural and geographical sphere than the Norwegian bunads.

We do not know of any folk costume tradition among the non-Lapp population in Finnmark. When Finnmark was burned to the ground during the war, in 1944, also old garments were destroyed. When Norwegian women in Finnmark wanted their own bunad, there was almost no material to build on. Finnmark Husflidslag took a look at the bunad question in 1954. The outcome was not very satisfying. But in 1967 the work on the Finnmark bunad was finished and the first bunads appeared.

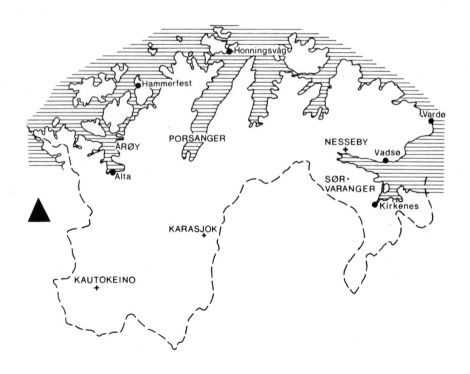

«Main street, Hammerfest, Finnmark». From: «Travels to Scandinavia, Lappland, Spitsbergen and the Faroese, 1838, 1839 and 1840». From «Atlas Pittoresque, volume I». Paris, France, 1852.

Woman's bunad from Finnmark

Finnmark Husflidslag designed the woman's bunad from Finnmark in 1967. It is a formal costume for non-Samic women so they did not have much of a tradition to build upon, because there are no folk costume traditions among the Norwegian population in Finnmark. The bodice was copied after an antique jacket from Tromsø Museum. The hat was copied after a tucked, styled hat from Porsanger, which was in use up until the Second World War. The whitework pattern on the blouse is copied from a «skalle-bånd», Samic booth trim. However the pattern was not of Samic origin. The bunad silver is copied after an antique brooch from Årøy in the Altafjord.

The skirt is made of black or dark blue wool material with a thin red band around the hem and above this, one green band and one rust band. It is pleated with a plain panel in front. The bodice is made of red wool material and with a peplum. It closes in front with silver hooks. A silver pendant is fastened with a silver hook on each side of the bodice. The blouse is made of white linen with whitework around the collar and the cuffs of the sleeves. It has a hat made of the same material and color as the skirt. The front piece has a red wool lining. A cape is used for the outdoors. Black stockings and black shoes are part of the costume. The silver for the Finnmark bunad does not have a traditional design. An antique bronze pendant was used as a copy for the neck pin, button cufflinks, silver hooks and the pendant.

BUNAD CUSTOMS

The bunads are very different from the clothes normally worn. They are either copies of garments belonging to a past area, or made as costumes for festive occasions. It is, therefore, quite necessary to become acquainted with how the individual bunads should be worn and used.

The fact that we have rules for the use of bunads does not necessarily mean any standardization of these costumes. Also in the old society, where the folk costumes belonged, there were many unwritten rules for use of the costumes. But the control exercised by customs is not always applicable today, because most owners of bunads only wear them once in awhile, and, in addition, the bunads are often used far away from the districts in which they originate. Many people, therefore, need advice on the usage of the bunads. Not so many years ago the then Miss Norway was photographed abroad with her Setesdal skirt turned the wrong way!

There is nothing wrong with copying some of the variations we know there were in folk costumes, both in shape, colors and combination of the individual garment pieces. The essential point is that the variations of the bunad usage must be justified on the basis of older costume material. When there are numerous plastrons in Hordaland, there is no reason to select only one pattern for a specific bunad. For the Sør-Østerdal bunad, one may choose between several jackets, bodices and shirts. All these pieces are, of course, copied from old costume garments.

A bunad is a costume for festive and holiday occasions, and is also considered quite proper as a gala attire. It is the festive folk costumes which live on in the bunads. In the old days there was a real difference between everyday wear and festive costumes.

Just as one would not use a formal garment for kitchen or office work, one would find it equally unthinkable to sit down at the spinning wheel or the loom in the finest garments meant for church. Thus bunads belong to festive and solemn occassions.

To really become a true festive costume it is important that the bunad is made of first class materials and by experts. In some districts a certain amount of control with the bunad assembly is exercised.

It is also important that the bunad fits. It has to be the right size. In that respect there is no difference between the bunad and other garments we use. The bunads are normally sewn in such a way that they can be let out or taken in.

The **bunad bodices** must be form-fitting and not too long. Klara Semb followed the very practical rule that the bunad bodice was to begin two fingers above the waistline.

Nor must the **bunad skirt** be too long. In the old days, the rule was that the road was not to be swept by the skirt. On the other hand, it must not be too short. The bunad skirt hem should be about 8—12 inches above the floor.

In order to do full justice to the skirt, an **underskirt** must be worn. One may well use a couple of underskirts, made from a very sturdy fabric. In the old days women wore several underskirts at the same time. In Flesberg they even wore up to seven of them. The «next-to-the-top skirt» was

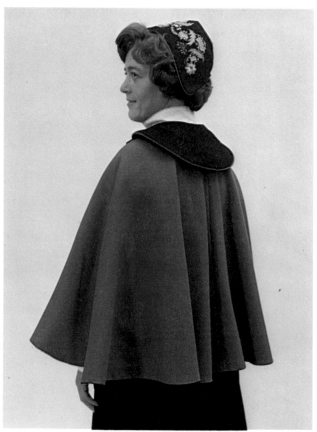

Here we show some samples of various types of top garments for women's bunads. Left: Woman's bunad from Lesja with wool shawl with printed pattern and fringes. The shawl is an heirloom from the 1700s. Right: For the woman's bunad from Østfold is worn a short, turnable cape of black and green wool material.

231

usually made of linen. It was the underskirt that was seen when the top skirt was rolled up to save wear and tear.

The **jacket** was for everyday as well as festive wear. In several districts one was not supposed to go to church without it, that is, in shirtsleeves. In Røros the bunad is never worn without a jacket. The jacket is an inseparable part of most of the bunads which are deeply rooted in old dress customs.

A bunad is a **complete** costume, composed of different pieces of garments. All pieces belong together.

Practically every bunad has a **kerchief**. In some areas there are different kerchiefs for married and unmarried women, a custom which deserves to be preserved. Kerchiefs are to be worn inside as well as outside the house at all times. No other headpiece should be worn together with the bunad, such as the caps worn by students and choir members. If one finds that the bunad kerchief does not fit one's hair style, one should modify the hair style to fit the bunad.

Black or colored **stockings** and **black bunad shoes** with metal clasps are obligatory for the woman's bunad. As for the man's bunad the stockings may vary somewhat more. For the folk costumes, handmade shoes and homespun stockings in various colors were used. In Telemark, the women wore embroidered homespun socks. Nowadays they are too impractical. Today it is almost impossible to find copies of old, handmade shoes. Black bunad shoes with metal clasps are, therefore, a practical solution to the problem. High-heeled, light or colored shoes, with or without heel and toe, should not under any circumstances be used with a bunad.

Many bunads have a special outer garment. In the old days, one wore a cape as well as a shawl. We here feature a selection of outer garments for various bunads. Regular coats do not «go» with bunads. In addition, they also «ruin» white shirtsleeves.

The **bunad silver** is a part of the bunad. Several bunads have their own bunad silver based on local silversmith art. Local traditions should be maintained also for the bunad silver. Registrations of old silver shows there is a wealth of material to draw from.

The wearing of costume silver was also subject to custom. We find different rules for how much silver the married and the unmarried women were allowed to wear. In Hardanger and Voss only married women were permitted to wear the «valley chain» and «chalet belt». Brooches and clasps have had their designated place on the bunad. It was only for weddings that lots of silver was worn. On the other hand, a bride could be lavishly adorned with silver.

It is up to each and everyone what bunad to wear. But usually one selects the bunad belonging to one's place of birth, or the district in where one lives.

Left: Checkered wool shawl with fringes used as top garment for the woman's bunad from Kvinnherad. Center: Woman's bunad from Sør-Østerdal with semi-long cape in red or blue patterned wool material. Right: Girl's bunad from Hardanger with long cape in dark wool fabric. This type of cape is in use in many places. Below: Traditional handmade shoes and embroidered homespun socks for women bunads in Telemark, here used for the «Sash costume». Nowadays very few are wearing these items.

CONTENTS

236